VB.NET SOURCE CODE: WBEMSCRIPTING GET

Richard Edwards

CONTENTS

INTRODUCTION

This book is constructed in a rather unique way.

Most books are, by nature, are written by subject experts who are very good at what they do. Very few are written by real programmers.

Programmers are the druids of computer programming. They tend to be soft spoken and easy going. Very focused and not wandering far from the computer keyboard.

I am neither one.

I am a writer who has been a programmer, developer and a solution expert for over the past 30 years. And as such, I am wanting to share my work with you in a rather unique way.

The book was written around the work contained in one module that from top to bottom comes out to 1850 lines of tested and reusable code. It was written in roughly 2 hours and it will take me the better part of a day for me to explain what each routine does and how you can make the routine more robust.

I can't do all of the work for you. Your own personal touch can go a long- ways.

There are also 10 pages of code which will help you create a physical overview of all namespaces and classes that is currently on your dev box. Beyond that, the rest of the work in this book is designed to be called by a form with the intent to produce reusable code.

Unfortunately, many of the routines in this book are also dedicated in that they must be used by the Win32_Process. But you can and should be able to see where changing the word Process to Bios, ComputerSystem, Product, or over 700 other names can easily turn the routines into something else entirely different.

WHAT WMI NAMESPACES AND CLASSES ARE ON YOUR MACHINE?

Someone once said, "It is what you don't know that can kill you," Well, they might not have said it exactly that way, but you get the idea.

How can you use something that exists on your machine, but you don't know it?

Back in 2002, I created something called the WMI Explorer. Microsoft came out with their version in May of 2003. Neither one of us cared, It pretty much fell flat on its face.

The biggest difference between the two is my class groupings was based on the way the classes were presented. In-other-words, I there was no underscore, the category was the classname. If there was an underscore at the beginning of the classname, it was a superclass. It there was an underscore in the middle of the classname, the letters before the underscore became its category.

I thought it was a pretty good idea at the time.

Apparently, no one else did. Fact is, the concept was never used by anyone else and WMI Explorer that other people began to "create" used the Microsoft template and never did consider a more granular approach.

I also think the other reason why the WMI Explorer didn't become popular was because of the lack of documentation beyond the most common root: root\cimv2. And back in 2003 time, there were less than a few hundred of them.

But today is a completely different ballpark. Today there are literally hundreds of classes under root\cimv2 alone.

Would you like your own personal copy?

The following scripts that I've been using since 2002, will make that happen for you. Just create a folder on your desktop, then copy and paste the three scripts into that directory and start with namespaces.vbs and end with classes.vbs.

NAMESPACES.VBS

```
Dim fso
Dim l
Dim s


EnumNamespaces("root")

Sub EnumNamespaces(ByVal nspace)

Set ws = CreateObject("Wscript.Shell")
Set fso = CreateObject("Scripting.FilesystemObject")

If fso.folderExists(ws.currentDirectory & "\" & nspace) = false then
fso.CreateFolder(ws.currentDirectory & "\" & nspace)
End If

On error Resume Next

Set        objs        =        GetObject("Winmgmts:\\.\"        &
nspace).InstancesOf("___Namespace", &H20000)

If err.Number <> 0 Then
err.Clear
Exit Sub
End If

For each obj in objs
```

```
EnumNamespaces(nspace & "\" & obj.Name)
Next

End Sub
```

Categories.VBS

```
Dim fso
Dim l
Dim s

Set ws = CreateObject("Wscript.Shell")
Set fso = CreateObject("Scripting.FilesystemObject")

EnumNamespaces("root")


Sub EnumNamespaces(ByVal nspace)

EnumCategories(nspace)

If fso.folderExists(ws.currentDirectory & "\" & nspace) = false then
fso.CreateFolder(ws.currentDirectory & "\" & nspace)
End If

On error Resume Next

Set        objs        =        GetObject("Winmgmts:\\.\"        &
nspace).InstancesOf("___Namespace", &H20000)

If err.Number <> 0 Then
err.Clear
Exit Sub
```

```
End If

For each obj in objs

EnumNamespaces(nspace & "\" & obj.Name)

Next

End Sub

Sub EnumCategories(ByVal nspace)

Set ws = CreateObject("Wscript.Shell")
Set fso = CreateObject("Scripting.FilesystemObject")

Set objs = GetObject("Winmgmts:\\.\" & nspace).SubClassesOf("", &H20000)
For each obj in objs

pos = instr(obj.Path_.class, "_")

if pos = 0 then
If fso.folderExists(ws.currentDirectory & "\" & nspace & "\" & obj.Path_.Class)
= false then
fso.CreateFolder(ws.currentDirectory & "\" & nspace & "\" & obj.Path_.Class)
End If
else
if pos = 1 then
If fso.folderExists(ws.currentDirectory & "\" & nspace & "\SuperClasses") =
false then
fso.CreateFolder(ws.currentDirectory & "\" & nspace & "\SuperClasses")
End If
else
```

```
     If   fso.folderExists(ws.currentDirectory   &   "\"   &   nspace   &   "\"   &
Mid(obj.Path_.Class, 1, pos-1)) = false then
     fso.CreateFolder(ws.currentDirectory   &   "\"   &   nspace   &   "\"   &
Mid(obj.Path_.Class, 1, pos-1))
     End If
     End If
     End If

     Next

     End Sub
```

Classes.VBS

```
     Dim fso
     Dim l
     Dim s

     EnumNamespaces("root")

     Sub EnumNamespaces(ByVal nspace)

     EnumClasses(nspace)

     Set ws = CreateObject("Wscript.Shell")
     Set fso = CreateObject("Scripting.FilesystemObject")

     If fso.folderExists(ws.currentDirectory & "\" & nspace) = false then
     fso.CreateFolder(ws.currentDirectory & "\" & nspace)
     End If

     On error Resume Next
```

```
Set       objs       =       GetObject("Winmgmts:\\.\"       &
nspace).InstancesOf("___Namespace", &H20000)

    If err.Number <> 0 Then
    err.Clear
    Exit Sub
    End If

    For each obj in objs

    EnumNamespaces(nspace & "\" & obj.Name)

    Next

    End Sub

    Sub EnumClasses(ByVal nspace)

    Set ws = CreateObject("Wscript.Shell")
    Set fso = CreateObject("Scripting.FilesystemObject")

    Set objs = GetObject("Winmgmts:\\.\" & nspace).SubClassesOf("", &H20000)
    For each obj in objs

    pos = instr(obj.Path_.class, "_")

    if pos = 0 then
    call   CreateXMLFile(ws.CurrentDirectory   &   "\"   &   nspace   &   "\"   &
obj.Path_.Class, nspace, obj.Path_.Class)
    else
    if pos = 1 then
```

```
            call  CreateXMlFile(ws.CurrentDirectory & "\" & nspace & "\Superclasses",
nspace, obj.Path_.Class)
            else
            call   CreateXMLFile(ws.CurrentDirectory  &   "\"  &   nspace  &   "\"  &
Mid(obj.Path_.Class, 1, pos-1), nspace, obj.Path_.Class)
            End If
            End If

            Next

            End Sub

            Sub CreateXMLFile(ByVal Path, ByVal nspace, ByVal ClassName)



            Set fso = CreateObject("Scripting.FileSystemObject")
            Dim shorty
            On error Resume Next
            shorty = fso.GetFolder(Path).ShortPath
            If err.Number <> 0 then
            err.Clear
            Exit Sub
            End IF



            set obj = GetObject("Winmgmts:\\.\" & nspace).Get(classname)

            Set txtstream = fso.OpenTextFile(Shorty & "\" & Classname & ".xml", 2, true, -
2)
            txtstream.WriteLine("<data>")
            txtstream.WriteLine(" <NamespaceInformation>")
            txtstream.WriteLine("   <namespace>" & nspace & "</namespace>")
```

```vb
txtstream.WriteLine("    <classname>" & classname & "</classname>")
txtstream.WriteLine("  </NamespaceInformation>")
txtstream.WriteLine("  <properties>")

for each prop in obj.Properties_
txtstream.WriteLine("        <property Name = """ & prop.Name & """ IsArray=""" & prop.IsArray & """ DataType = """ & prop.Qualifiers_("CIMType").Value & """/>")
Next
txtstream.WriteLine("  </properties>")
txtstream.WriteLine("</data>")
txtstream.close

End sub
```

As shown below, once these routines are done, you should be able to go to the folder, based on what I've told you about the Namespace\category\classes

File | Home | Share | View

Directory ▸ root ▸ CIMV2 ▸ Win32

Favorites
- Desktop
- Downloads
- Recent places

This PC
- Desktop
- Documents
- Downloads
- Music
- Pictures
- Videos
- Local Disk (C:)
- DVD RW Drive (D:) DN600ENU2
- Local Disk (E:)
- Powershell Basic Examples (F:)
- New Volume (G:)
- New Volume (H:)

Network
- WDMYCLOUD
- WDMYCLOUD1
- WIN-SJRLOAKMF5B
- WIN-VNQ7KUKQ4NE

Name	Date modified	Type
Win32_1394Controller	6/5/2018 6:41 PM	XML File
Win32_1394ControllerDevice	6/5/2018 6:41 PM	XML File
Win32_Account	6/5/2018 6:41 PM	XML File
Win32_AccountSID	6/5/2018 6:41 PM	XML File
Win32_ACE	6/5/2018 6:41 PM	XML File
Win32_ActionCheck	6/5/2018 6:42 PM	XML File
Win32_ActiveRoute	6/5/2018 6:41 PM	XML File
Win32_AllocatedResource	6/5/2018 6:41 PM	XML File
Win32_ApplicationCommandLine	6/5/2018 6:41 PM	XML File
Win32_ApplicationService	6/5/2018 6:41 PM	XML File
Win32_AssociatedProcessorMemory	6/5/2018 6:41 PM	XML File
Win32_AutochkSetting	6/5/2018 6:41 PM	XML File
Win32_BaseBoard	6/5/2018 6:41 PM	XML File
Win32_BaseService	6/5/2018 6:41 PM	XML File
Win32_Battery	6/5/2018 6:41 PM	XML File
Win32_Binary	6/5/2018 6:41 PM	XML File
Win32_BindImageAction	6/5/2018 6:41 PM	XML File
Win32_BIOS	6/5/2018 6:41 PM	XML File
Win32_BootConfiguration	6/5/2018 6:41 PM	XML File
Win32_Bus	6/5/2018 6:41 PM	XML File
Win32_CacheMemory	6/5/2018 6:41 PM	XML File
Win32_CDROMDrive	6/5/2018 6:41 PM	XML File
Win32_CheckCheck	6/5/2018 6:42 PM	XML File
Win32_CIMLogicalDeviceCIMDataFile	6/5/2018 6:41 PM	XML File
Win32_ClassicCOMApplicationClasses	6/5/2018 6:41 PM	XML File

686 items

And If you open one of these up:

- <data>
  - <NamespaceInformation>
      <namespace>root\CIMV2</namespace>
      <classname>Win32_BIOS</classname>
    </NamespaceInformation>
  - <properties>
      <property Name="BiosCharacteristics" IsArray="True" DataType="uint16"/>
      <property Name="BIOSVersion" IsArray="True" DataType="string"/>
      <property Name="BuildNumber" IsArray="False" DataType="string"/>
      <property Name="Caption" IsArray="False" DataType="string"/>
      <property Name="CodeSet" IsArray="False" DataType="string"/>
      <property Name="CurrentLanguage" IsArray="False" DataType="string"/>
      <property Name="Description" IsArray="False" DataType="string"/>
      <property Name="IdentificationCode" IsArray="False" DataType="string"/>
      <property Name="InstallableLanguages" IsArray="False" DataType="uint16"/>
      <property Name="InstallDate" IsArray="False" DataType="datetime"/>
      <property Name="LanguageEdition" IsArray="False" DataType="string"/>
      <property Name="ListOfLanguages" IsArray="True" DataType="string"/>
      <property Name="Manufacturer" IsArray="False" DataType="string"/>
      <property Name="Name" IsArray="False" DataType="string"/>
      <property Name="OtherTargetOS" IsArray="False" DataType="string"/>
      <property Name="PrimaryBIOS" IsArray="False" DataType="boolean"/>
      <property Name="ReleaseDate" IsArray="False" DataType="datetime"/>
      <property Name="SerialNumber" IsArray="False" DataType="string"/>
      <property Name="SMBIOSBIOSVersion" IsArray="False" DataType="string"/>
      <property Name="SMBIOSMajorVersion" IsArray="False" DataType="uint16"/>
      <property Name="SMBIOSMinorVersion" IsArray="False" DataType="uint16"/>
      <property Name="SMBIOSPresent" IsArray="False" DataType="boolean"/>
      <property Name="SoftwareElementID" IsArray="False" DataType="string"/>
      <property Name="SoftwareElementState" IsArray="False" DataType="uint16"/>
      <property Name="Status" IsArray="False" DataType="string"/>
      <property Name="TargetOperatingSystem" IsArray="False" DataType="uint16"/>
      <property Name="Version" IsArray="False" DataType="string"/>
    </properties>
  </data>

GETTING STARTED

Whether you are using Visual Studio 2010 or higher, the first thing you're going to want to do is create a new Windows Application project in Vb.Net. The second thing you're going to need to do is make a reference the COM namespace. Now, add a module to your project and then, above the name of the module, add the imports statement that is shown below.

```
Imports WbemScripting
Module Module1
```

DECLARING VARIABLES

As you can see from the below code, we are enabling the use of specific variables and objects at the very top of the module ns is made public so that the form can specify what WMI namespace will be used by the program along with what class will be called upon to provide us with information about your local machine. The old school version of the FileSystem Object is created along with an empty object we're going to be using as the textstream.

```
Public ns As String
Public Classname As String
Public fso As Object = CreateObject("Scripting.FileSystemObject")
Public txtstream As Object
```

THE GETVALUE FUNCTION

This is where a function called GetValue is the very first routine of the module and is used to return the value of the property in the row of an object collection. One of the first things I learned early on is that it is much easier to parse a string than to have to deal with converting a laundry list of property datatypes and react to the common datetime datatype. Either there is a value assigned to the Property or there isn't. Either that value is a datetime datatype or it isn't.

```
Public Function GetValue(ByVal Name As String, ByVal obj As
SWbemObject) As String

        Dim PName As String = Chr(9) + Name + " = "
        Dim tempstr As String = obj.GetObjectText_
        Dim pos As Integer = tempstr.IndexOf(PName)
        If pos > 0 Then

            pos = pos + PName.Length
            tempstr = tempstr.Substring(pos, (tempstr.Length -
pos))
            pos = tempstr.IndexOf(";")
            tempstr = tempstr.Substring(0, pos)
            tempstr = tempstr.Replace(Chr(34), "")
            tempstr = tempstr.Replace("}", "")
            tempstr = tempstr.Replace("{", "")
            tempstr = tempstr.Trim()
            If tempstr.Length > 14 Then

                If obj.Properties_.Item(Name).CIMType =
WbemCimtypeEnum.wbemCimtypeDatetime Then

                    Dim tstr As String = tempstr.Substring(4, 2)
                    tstr = tstr + "/"
                    tstr = tstr + tempstr.Substring(6, 2)
                    tstr = tstr + "/"
                    tstr = tstr + tempstr.Substring(0, 4)
```

```
                    tstr = tstr + " "
                    tstr = tstr + tempstr.Substring(8, 2)
                    tstr = tstr + ":"
                    tstr = tstr + tempstr.Substring(10, 2)
                    tstr = tstr + ":"
                    tstr = tstr + tempstr.Substring(12, 2)
                    tempstr = tstr

            End If
        End If

        Return tempstr

    Else

        Return ""

    End If

End Function
```

RETURN A SWBEMOBJECTSET

The purpose of this function is to return a collection of objects and properties we can use to populate and view in a variety of formats and orientations.

```
Public Function Return_SWbemObjectSet() As SWbemObjectSet

    Dim l As WbemScripting.SWbemLocator = New
WbemScripting.SWbemLocator
    Dim svc As SWbemServices = l.ConnectServer(".", ns, "",
"", "MS_0409")
    svc.Security_.AuthenticationLevel =
WbemAuthenticationLevelEnum.wbemAuthenticationLevelPktPrivacy
    svc.Security_.ImpersonationLevel =
WbemImpersonationLevelEnum.wbemImpersonationLevelImpersonate
    Dim ob As SWbemObject = svc.Get(Classname)
    Dim objs As SWbemObjectSet = ob.Instances_

    Return objs

End Function
```

CREATE ASP CODE

Inside this sub routine is the code to create an ASP Webpage. You simply pass in the collection generated by the Return_Management_Collection and specify its orientation.

```
Public Sub Create_ASP_Code(ByVal objs As SWbemObjectSet, ByVal Orientation
As String)


txtstream          =          fso.OpenTextFile(Application.StartupPath          +
"\\Win32_Process.asp", 2, True, -2)
    txtstream.WriteLine("<html xmlns=""http://www.w3.org/1999/xhtml"">")
    txtstream.WriteLine("<head>")
    txtstream.WriteLine("<head>")
    txtstream.WriteLine("<style type='text/css'>")
    txtstream.WriteLine("body")
    txtstream.WriteLine("{")
    txtstream.WriteLine("   PADDING-RIGHT: 0px;")
    txtstream.WriteLine("   PADDING-LEFT: 0px;")
    txtstream.WriteLine("   PADDING-BOTTOM: 0px;")
    txtstream.WriteLine("   MARGIN: 0px;")
    txtstream.WriteLine("   COLOR: #333;")
    txtstream.WriteLine("   PADDING-TOP: 0px;")
    txtstream.WriteLine("   FONT-FAMILY: verdana, arial, helvetica, sans-serif;")
    txtstream.WriteLine("}")
    txtstream.WriteLine("table")
    txtstream.WriteLine("{")
    txtstream.WriteLine("   BORDER-RIGHT: #999999 1px solid;")
```

```
txtstream.WriteLine("   PADDING-RIGHT: 1px;")
txtstream.WriteLine("   PADDING-LEFT: 1px;")
txtstream.WriteLine("   PADDING-BOTTOM: 1px;")
txtstream.WriteLine("   LINE-HEIGHT: 8px;")
txtstream.WriteLine("   PADDING-TOP: 1px;")
txtstream.WriteLine("   BORDER-BOTTOM: #999 1px solid;")
txtstream.WriteLine("   BACKGROUND-COLOR: #eeeeee;")
txtstream.WriteLine("
filter:progid:DXImageTransform.Microsoft.Shadow(color='silver',      Direction=135,
Strength=16)")
txtstream.WriteLine("}")
txtstream.WriteLine("th")
txtstream.WriteLine("{")
txtstream.WriteLine("   BORDER-RIGHT: #999999 3px solid;")
txtstream.WriteLine("   PADDING-RIGHT: 6px;")
txtstream.WriteLine("   PADDING-LEFT: 6px;")
txtstream.WriteLine("   FONT-WEIGHT: Bold;")
txtstream.WriteLine("   FONT-SIZE: 14px;")
txtstream.WriteLine("   PADDING-BOTTOM: 6px;")
txtstream.WriteLine("   COLOR: darkred;")
txtstream.WriteLine("   LINE-HEIGHT: 14px;")
txtstream.WriteLine("   PADDING-TOP: 6px;")
txtstream.WriteLine("   BORDER-BOTTOM: #999 1px solid;")
txtstream.WriteLine("   BACKGROUND-COLOR: #eeeeee;")
txtstream.WriteLine("   FONT-FAMILY: font-family: Cambria, serif;")
txtstream.WriteLine("   FONT-SIZE: 12px;")
txtstream.WriteLine("   text-align: left;")
txtstream.WriteLine("   white-Space: nowrap;")
txtstream.WriteLine("}")
txtstream.WriteLine(".th")
txtstream.WriteLine("{")
txtstream.WriteLine("   BORDER-RIGHT: #999999 2px solid;")
txtstream.WriteLine("   PADDING-RIGHT: 6px;")
```

```
txtstream.WriteLine("    PADDING-LEFT: 6px;")
txtstream.WriteLine("    FONT-WEIGHT: Bold;")
txtstream.WriteLine("    PADDING-BOTTOM: 6px;")
txtstream.WriteLine("    COLOR: black;")
txtstream.WriteLine("    PADDING-TOP: 6px;")
txtstream.WriteLine("    BORDER-BOTTOM: #999 2px solid;")
txtstream.WriteLine("    BACKGROUND-COLOR: #eeeeee;")
txtstream.WriteLine("    FONT-FAMILY: font-family: Cambria, serif;")
txtstream.WriteLine("    FONT-SIZE: 10px;")
txtstream.WriteLine("    text-align: right;")
txtstream.WriteLine("    white-Space: nowrap;")
txtstream.WriteLine("}")
txtstream.WriteLine("td")
txtstream.WriteLine("{")
txtstream.WriteLine("    BORDER-RIGHT: #999999 3px solid;")
txtstream.WriteLine("    PADDING-RIGHT: 6px;")
txtstream.WriteLine("    PADDING-LEFT: 6px;")
txtstream.WriteLine("    FONT-WEIGHT: Normal;")
txtstream.WriteLine("    PADDING-BOTTOM: 6px;")
txtstream.WriteLine("    COLOR: navy;")
txtstream.WriteLine("    LINE-HEIGHT: 14px;")
txtstream.WriteLine("    PADDING-TOP: 6px;")
txtstream.WriteLine("    BORDER-BOTTOM: #999 1px solid;")
txtstream.WriteLine("    BACKGROUND-COLOR: #eeeeee;")
txtstream.WriteLine("    FONT-FAMILY: font-family: Cambria, serif;")
txtstream.WriteLine("    FONT-SIZE: 12px;")
txtstream.WriteLine("    text-align: left;")
txtstream.WriteLine("    white-Space: nowrap;")
txtstream.WriteLine("}")
txtstream.WriteLine("div")
txtstream.WriteLine("{")
txtstream.WriteLine("    BORDER-RIGHT: #999999 3px solid;")
txtstream.WriteLine("    PADDING-RIGHT: 6px;")
```

```
txtstream.WriteLine("    PADDING-LEFT: 6px;")
txtstream.WriteLine("    FONT-WEIGHT: Normal;")
txtstream.WriteLine("    PADDING-BOTTOM: 6px;")
txtstream.WriteLine("    COLOR: white;")
txtstream.WriteLine("    PADDING-TOP: 6px;")
txtstream.WriteLine("    BORDER-BOTTOM: #999 1px solid;")
txtstream.WriteLine("    BACKGROUND-COLOR: navy;")
txtstream.WriteLine("    FONT-FAMILY: font-family: Cambria, serif;")
txtstream.WriteLine("    FONT-SIZE: 10px;")
txtstream.WriteLine("    text-align: left;")
txtstream.WriteLine("    white-Space: nowrap;")
txtstream.WriteLine("}")
txtstream.WriteLine("span")
txtstream.WriteLine("{")
txtstream.WriteLine("    BORDER-RIGHT: #999999 3px solid;")
txtstream.WriteLine("    PADDING-RIGHT: 3px;")
txtstream.WriteLine("    PADDING-LEFT: 3px;")
txtstream.WriteLine("    FONT-WEIGHT: Normal;")
txtstream.WriteLine("    PADDING-BOTTOM: 3px;")
txtstream.WriteLine("    COLOR: white;")
txtstream.WriteLine("    PADDING-TOP: 3px;")
txtstream.WriteLine("    BORDER-BOTTOM: #999 1px solid;")
txtstream.WriteLine("    BACKGROUND-COLOR: navy;")
txtstream.WriteLine("    FONT-FAMILY: font-family: Cambria, serif;")
txtstream.WriteLine("    FONT-SIZE: 10px;")
txtstream.WriteLine("    text-align: left;")
txtstream.WriteLine("    white-Space: nowrap;")
txtstream.WriteLine("    display: inline-block;")
txtstream.WriteLine("    width: 100%;")
txtstream.WriteLine("}")
txtstream.WriteLine("textarea")
txtstream.WriteLine("{")
txtstream.WriteLine("    BORDER-RIGHT: #999999 3px solid;")
```

```
txtstream.WriteLine("    PADDING-RIGHT: 3px;")
txtstream.WriteLine("    PADDING-LEFT: 3px;")
txtstream.WriteLine("    FONT-WEIGHT: Normal;")
txtstream.WriteLine("    PADDING-BOTTOM: 3px;")
txtstream.WriteLine("    COLOR: white;")
txtstream.WriteLine("    PADDING-TOP: 3px;")
txtstream.WriteLine("    BORDER-BOTTOM: #999 1px solid;")
txtstream.WriteLine("    BACKGROUND-COLOR: navy;")
txtstream.WriteLine("    FONT-FAMILY: font-family: Cambria, serif;")
txtstream.WriteLine("    FONT-SIZE: 10px;")
txtstream.WriteLine("    text-align: left;")
txtstream.WriteLine("    white-Space: nowrap;")
txtstream.WriteLine("    width: 100%;")
txtstream.WriteLine("}")
txtstream.WriteLine("select")
txtstream.WriteLine("{")
txtstream.WriteLine("    BORDER-RIGHT: #999999 3px solid;")
txtstream.WriteLine("    PADDING-RIGHT: 6px;")
txtstream.WriteLine("    PADDING-LEFT: 6px;")
txtstream.WriteLine("    FONT-WEIGHT: Normal;")
txtstream.WriteLine("    PADDING-BOTTOM: 6px;")
txtstream.WriteLine("    COLOR: white;")
txtstream.WriteLine("    PADDING-TOP: 6px;")
txtstream.WriteLine("    BORDER-BOTTOM: #999 1px solid;")
txtstream.WriteLine("    BACKGROUND-COLOR: navy;")
txtstream.WriteLine("    FONT-FAMILY: font-family: Cambria, serif;")
txtstream.WriteLine("    FONT-SIZE: 10px;")
txtstream.WriteLine("    text-align: left;")
txtstream.WriteLine("    white-Space: nowrap;")
txtstream.WriteLine("    width: 100%;")
txtstream.WriteLine("}")
txtstream.WriteLine("input")
txtstream.WriteLine("{")
```

```
txtstream.WriteLine("   BORDER-RIGHT: #999999 3px solid;")
txtstream.WriteLine("   PADDING-RIGHT: 3px;")
txtstream.WriteLine("   PADDING-LEFT: 3px;")
txtstream.WriteLine("   FONT-WEIGHT: Bold;")
txtstream.WriteLine("   PADDING-BOTTOM: 3px;")
txtstream.WriteLine("   COLOR: white;")
txtstream.WriteLine("   PADDING-TOP: 3px;")
txtstream.WriteLine("   BORDER-BOTTOM: #999 1px solid;")
txtstream.WriteLine("   BACKGROUND-COLOR: navy;")
txtstream.WriteLine("   FONT-FAMILY: font-family: Cambria, serif;")
txtstream.WriteLine("   FONT-SIZE: 12px;")
txtstream.WriteLine("   text-align: left;")
txtstream.WriteLine("   display: table-cell;")
txtstream.WriteLine("   white-Space: nowrap;")
txtstream.WriteLine("   width: 100%;")
txtstream.WriteLine("}")
txtstream.WriteLine("h1 {")
txtstream.WriteLine("color: antiquewhite;")
txtstream.WriteLine("text-shadow: 1px 1px 1px black;")
txtstream.WriteLine("padding: 3px;")
txtstream.WriteLine("text-align: center;")
txtstream.WriteLine("box-shadow: inset 2px 2px 5px rgba(0,0,0,0.5), inset -
2px -2px 5px rgba(255,255,255,0.5)")
txtstream.WriteLine("}")
txtstream.WriteLine("</style>")
txtstream.WriteLine("<title>Win32_Process</title>")
txtstream.WriteLine("</head>")
txtstream.WriteLine("<body>")
txtstream.WriteLine("<%")
txtstream.WriteLine("Response.Write(""<table    Border='1'    cellpadding='1'
cellspacing='1'>"" & vbcrlf)")

Select Case Orientation
```

```vb
Case "Single-Line Horizontal"

Dim ob As Object = objs.ItemIndex(0)
txtstream.WriteLine("Response.Write(""<tr>"" & vbcrlf)")
For Each prop In ob.Properties_
txtstream.WriteLine("Response.Write(""<th>" + prop.Name + "</th>"" &
vbcrlf)")
Next
txtstream.WriteLine("Response.Write(""</tr>"" & vbcrlf)")
txtstream.WriteLine("Response.Write(""<tr>"" & vbcrlf)")
For Each prop As Object In ob.Properties_
Dim value As String = GetValue(prop.Name, ob)
txtstream.WriteLine("Response.Write(""<td>" + value + "</td>"" & vbcrlf)")
Next
txtstream.WriteLine("Response.Write(""</tr>"" & vbcrlf)")


Case "Multi-Line Horizontal"

Dim ob As Object = objs.ItemIndex(0)
txtstream.WriteLine("Response.Write(""<tr>"" & vbcrlf)")
For Each prop In ob.Properties_
txtstream.WriteLine("Response.Write(""<th>" + prop.Name + "</th>"" &
vbcrlf)")
Next
txtstream.WriteLine("Response.Write(""</tr>"" & vbcrlf)")
For Each obj As Object In objs
txtstream.WriteLine("Response.Write(""<tr>"" & vbcrlf)")
For Each prop As Object In obj.Properties_
Dim value As String = GetValue(prop.Name, obj)
txtstream.WriteLine("Response.Write(""<td>" + value + "</td>"" & vbcrlf)")
```

```
Next
txtstream.WriteLine("Response.Write(""</tr>""" & vbcrlf)")
Next


Case "Single-Line Vertical"


Dim ob As Object = objs.ItemIndex(0)

For Each prop In ob.Properties_
txtstream.WriteLine("Response.Write(""<tr><th>"     +     prop.Name     +
"</th><td>" + GetValue(prop.Name, ob) + "</td></tr>""" & vbcrlf)")
Next



Case "Multi-Line Vertical"


Dim ob As Object = objs.ItemIndex(0)
For Each prop In ob.Properties_
txtstream.WriteLine("Response.Write(""<tr><th>" + prop.Name + "</th>""" &
vbcrlf)")
For Each obj As Object In objs
txtstream.WriteLine("Response.Write(""<td>"     +     GetValue(prop.name, obj) +
"</td>""" & vbcrlf)")
Next
txtstream.WriteLine("Response.Write(""</tr>""" & vbcrlf)")
Next



End Select


txtstream.WriteLine("Response.Write(""</table>""" & vbcrlf)")
```

```
txtstream.WriteLine("%>")
txtstream.WriteLine("</body>")
txtstream.WriteLine("</html>")
txtstream.Close()

End Sub
```

CREATE ASPX CODE

Inside this sub routine is the code to create an ASPX Webpage. You simply pass in the collection generated by the Return_Management_Collection and specify its orientation.

Public Sub Create_ASPX_Code(ByVal objs As SWbemObjectSet, ByVal Orientation As String)

```
txtstream = fso.OpenTextFile(Application.StartupPath + "\\Win32_Process.aspx", 2, True, -2)
txtstream.WriteLine("<!DOCTYPE html PUBLIC ""-//W3C//DTD XHTML 1.0 Transitional//EN"" ""http://www.w3.org/TR/xhtml1/DTD/xhtml1-transitional.dtd"">")
txtstream.WriteLine("")
txtstream.WriteLine("<html xmlns=""http://www.w3.org/1999/xhtml"">")
txtstream.WriteLine("<head>")
txtstream.WriteLine("<style type='text/css'>")
txtstream.WriteLine("body")
txtstream.WriteLine("{")
txtstream.WriteLine("    PADDING-RIGHT: 0px;")
txtstream.WriteLine("    PADDING-LEFT: 0px;")
txtstream.WriteLine("    PADDING-BOTTOM: 0px;")
txtstream.WriteLine("    MARGIN: 0px;")
txtstream.WriteLine("    COLOR: #333;")
txtstream.WriteLine("    PADDING-TOP: 0px;")
txtstream.WriteLine("    FONT-FAMILY: verdana, arial, helvetica, sans-serif;")
```

```
txtstream.WriteLine("}")
txtstream.WriteLine("table")
txtstream.WriteLine("{")
txtstream.WriteLine("    BORDER-RIGHT: #999999 1px solid;")
txtstream.WriteLine("    PADDING-RIGHT: 1px;")
txtstream.WriteLine("    PADDING-LEFT: 1px;")
txtstream.WriteLine("    PADDING-BOTTOM: 1px;")
txtstream.WriteLine("    LINE-HEIGHT: 8px;")
txtstream.WriteLine("    PADDING-TOP: 1px;")
txtstream.WriteLine("    BORDER-BOTTOM: #999 1px solid;")
txtstream.WriteLine("    BACKGROUND-COLOR: #eeeeee;")
txtstream.WriteLine("
filter:progid:DXImageTransform.Microsoft.Shadow(color='silver',    Direction=135,
Strength=16)")
txtstream.WriteLine("}")
txtstream.WriteLine("th")
txtstream.WriteLine("{")
txtstream.WriteLine("    BORDER-RIGHT: #999999 3px solid;")
txtstream.WriteLine("    PADDING-RIGHT: 6px;")
txtstream.WriteLine("    PADDING-LEFT: 6px;")
txtstream.WriteLine("    FONT-WEIGHT: Bold;")
txtstream.WriteLine("    FONT-SIZE: 14px;")
txtstream.WriteLine("    PADDING-BOTTOM: 6px;")
txtstream.WriteLine("    COLOR: darkred;")
txtstream.WriteLine("    LINE-HEIGHT: 14px;")
txtstream.WriteLine("    PADDING-TOP: 6px;")
txtstream.WriteLine("    BORDER-BOTTOM: #999 1px solid;")
txtstream.WriteLine("    BACKGROUND-COLOR: #eeeeee;")
txtstream.WriteLine("    FONT-FAMILY: font-family: Cambria, serif;")
txtstream.WriteLine("    FONT-SIZE: 12px;")
txtstream.WriteLine("    text-align: left;")
txtstream.WriteLine("    white-Space: nowrap;")
txtstream.WriteLine("}")
```

```
txtstream.WriteLine(".th")
txtstream.WriteLine("{")
txtstream.WriteLine("    BORDER-RIGHT: #999999 2px solid;")
txtstream.WriteLine("    PADDING-RIGHT: 6px;")
txtstream.WriteLine("    PADDING-LEFT: 6px;")
txtstream.WriteLine("    FONT-WEIGHT: Bold;")
txtstream.WriteLine("    PADDING-BOTTOM: 6px;")
txtstream.WriteLine("    COLOR: black;")
txtstream.WriteLine("    PADDING-TOP: 6px;")
txtstream.WriteLine("    BORDER-BOTTOM: #999 2px solid;")
txtstream.WriteLine("    BACKGROUND-COLOR: #eeeeee;")
txtstream.WriteLine("    FONT-FAMILY: font-family: Cambria, serif;")
txtstream.WriteLine("    FONT-SIZE: 10px;")
txtstream.WriteLine("    text-align: right;")
txtstream.WriteLine("    white-Space: nowrap;")
txtstream.WriteLine("}")
txtstream.WriteLine("td")
txtstream.WriteLine("{")
txtstream.WriteLine("    BORDER-RIGHT: #999999 3px solid;")
txtstream.WriteLine("    PADDING-RIGHT: 6px;")
txtstream.WriteLine("    PADDING-LEFT: 6px;")
txtstream.WriteLine("    FONT-WEIGHT: Normal;")
txtstream.WriteLine("    PADDING-BOTTOM: 6px;")
txtstream.WriteLine("    COLOR: navy;")
txtstream.WriteLine("    LINE-HEIGHT: 14px;")
txtstream.WriteLine("    PADDING-TOP: 6px;")
txtstream.WriteLine("    BORDER-BOTTOM: #999 1px solid;")
txtstream.WriteLine("    BACKGROUND-COLOR: #eeeeee;")
txtstream.WriteLine("    FONT-FAMILY: font-family: Cambria, serif;")
txtstream.WriteLine("    FONT-SIZE: 12px;")
txtstream.WriteLine("    text-align: left;")
txtstream.WriteLine("    white-Space: nowrap;")
txtstream.WriteLine("}")
```

```
txtstream.WriteLine("div")
txtstream.WriteLine("{")
txtstream.WriteLine("    BORDER-RIGHT: #999999 3px solid;")
txtstream.WriteLine("    PADDING-RIGHT: 6px;")
txtstream.WriteLine("    PADDING-LEFT: 6px;")
txtstream.WriteLine("    FONT-WEIGHT: Normal;")
txtstream.WriteLine("    PADDING-BOTTOM: 6px;")
txtstream.WriteLine("    COLOR: white;")
txtstream.WriteLine("    PADDING-TOP: 6px;")
txtstream.WriteLine("    BORDER-BOTTOM: #999 1px solid;")
txtstream.WriteLine("    BACKGROUND-COLOR: navy;")
txtstream.WriteLine("    FONT-FAMILY: font-family: Cambria, serif;")
txtstream.WriteLine("    FONT-SIZE: 10px;")
txtstream.WriteLine("    text-align: left;")
txtstream.WriteLine("    white-Space: nowrap;")
txtstream.WriteLine("}")
txtstream.WriteLine("span")
txtstream.WriteLine("{")
txtstream.WriteLine("    BORDER-RIGHT: #999999 3px solid;")
txtstream.WriteLine("    PADDING-RIGHT: 3px;")
txtstream.WriteLine("    PADDING-LEFT: 3px;")
txtstream.WriteLine("    FONT-WEIGHT: Normal;")
txtstream.WriteLine("    PADDING-BOTTOM: 3px;")
txtstream.WriteLine("    COLOR: white;")
txtstream.WriteLine("    PADDING-TOP: 3px;")
txtstream.WriteLine("    BORDER-BOTTOM: #999 1px solid;")
txtstream.WriteLine("    BACKGROUND-COLOR: navy;")
txtstream.WriteLine("    FONT-FAMILY: font-family: Cambria, serif;")
txtstream.WriteLine("    FONT-SIZE: 10px;")
txtstream.WriteLine("    text-align: left;")
txtstream.WriteLine("    white-Space: nowrap;")
txtstream.WriteLine("    display: inline-block;")
txtstream.WriteLine("    width: 100%;")
```

```
txtstream.WriteLine("}")
txtstream.WriteLine("textarea")
txtstream.WriteLine("{")
txtstream.WriteLine("    BORDER-RIGHT: #999999 3px solid;")
txtstream.WriteLine("    PADDING-RIGHT: 3px;")
txtstream.WriteLine("    PADDING-LEFT: 3px;")
txtstream.WriteLine("    FONT-WEIGHT: Normal;")
txtstream.WriteLine("    PADDING-BOTTOM: 3px;")
txtstream.WriteLine("    COLOR: white;")
txtstream.WriteLine("    PADDING-TOP: 3px;")
txtstream.WriteLine("    BORDER-BOTTOM: #999 1px solid;")
txtstream.WriteLine("    BACKGROUND-COLOR: navy;")
txtstream.WriteLine("    FONT-FAMILY: font-family: Cambria, serif;")
txtstream.WriteLine("    FONT-SIZE: 10px;")
txtstream.WriteLine("    text-align: left;")
txtstream.WriteLine("    white-Space: nowrap;")
txtstream.WriteLine("    width: 100%;")
txtstream.WriteLine("}")
txtstream.WriteLine("select")
txtstream.WriteLine("{")
txtstream.WriteLine("    BORDER-RIGHT: #999999 3px solid;")
txtstream.WriteLine("    PADDING-RIGHT: 6px;")
txtstream.WriteLine("    PADDING-LEFT: 6px;")
txtstream.WriteLine("    FONT-WEIGHT: Normal;")
txtstream.WriteLine("    PADDING-BOTTOM: 6px;")
txtstream.WriteLine("    COLOR: white;")
txtstream.WriteLine("    PADDING-TOP: 6px;")
txtstream.WriteLine("    BORDER-BOTTOM: #999 1px solid;")
txtstream.WriteLine("    BACKGROUND-COLOR: navy;")
txtstream.WriteLine("    FONT-FAMILY: font-family: Cambria, serif;")
txtstream.WriteLine("    FONT-SIZE: 10px;")
txtstream.WriteLine("    text-align: left;")
txtstream.WriteLine("    white-Space: nowrap;")
```

```
txtstream.WriteLine("    width: 100%;")
txtstream.WriteLine("}")
txtstream.WriteLine("input")
txtstream.WriteLine("{")
txtstream.WriteLine("    BORDER-RIGHT: #999999 3px solid;")
txtstream.WriteLine("    PADDING-RIGHT: 3px;")
txtstream.WriteLine("    PADDING-LEFT: 3px;")
txtstream.WriteLine("    FONT-WEIGHT: Bold;")
txtstream.WriteLine("    PADDING-BOTTOM: 3px;")
txtstream.WriteLine("    COLOR: white;")
txtstream.WriteLine("    PADDING-TOP: 3px;")
txtstream.WriteLine("    BORDER-BOTTOM: #999 1px solid;")
txtstream.WriteLine("    BACKGROUND-COLOR: navy;")
txtstream.WriteLine("    FONT-FAMILY: font-family: Cambria, serif;")
txtstream.WriteLine("    FONT-SIZE: 12px;")
txtstream.WriteLine("    text-align: left;")
txtstream.WriteLine("    display: table-cell;")
txtstream.WriteLine("    white-Space: nowrap;")
txtstream.WriteLine("    width: 100%;")
txtstream.WriteLine("}")
txtstream.WriteLine("h1 {")
txtstream.WriteLine("color: antiquewhite;")
txtstream.WriteLine("text-shadow: 1px 1px 1px black;")
txtstream.WriteLine("padding: 3px;")
txtstream.WriteLine("text-align: center;")
txtstream.WriteLine("box-shadow: inset 2px 2px 5px rgba(0,0,0,0.5), inset -2px -2px 5px rgba(255,255,255,0.5)")
txtstream.WriteLine("}")
txtstream.WriteLine("</style>")
txtstream.WriteLine("</head>")
txtstream.WriteLine("<body>")
txtstream.WriteLine("<%")
```

```
txtstream.WriteLine("Response.Write(""<table    Border='1'    cellpadding='1'
cellspacing='1'>"" & vbcrlf)")

Select Case Orientation


Case "Single-Line Horizontal"

Dim ob As Object = objs.ItemIndex(0)
txtstream.WriteLine("Response.Write(""<tr>"" & vbcrlf)")
For Each prop In ob.Properties_
txtstream.WriteLine("Response.Write(""<th>" + prop.Name + "</th>"" &
vbcrlf)")
Next
txtstream.WriteLine("Response.Write(""</tr>"" & vbcrlf)")
txtstream.WriteLine("Response.Write(""<tr>"" & vbcrlf)")
For Each prop As Object In ob.Properties_
Dim value As String = GetValue(prop.Name, ob)
txtstream.WriteLine("Response.Write(""<td>" + value + "</td>"" & vbcrlf)")
Next
txtstream.WriteLine("Response.Write(""</tr>"" & vbcrlf)")


Case "Multi-Line Horizontal"

Dim ob As Object = objs.ItemIndex(0)
txtstream.WriteLine("Response.Write(""<tr>"" & vbcrlf)")
For Each prop In ob.Properties_
txtstream.WriteLine("Response.Write(""<th>" + prop.Name + "</th>"" &
vbcrlf)")
Next
txtstream.WriteLine("Response.Write(""</tr>"" & vbcrlf)")
For Each obj As Object In objs
```

```vb
txtstream.WriteLine("Response.Write(""<tr>"" & vbcrlf)")
For Each prop As Object In obj.Properties_
Dim value As String = GetValue(prop.Name, obj)
txtstream.WriteLine("Response.Write(""<td>" + value + "</td>"" & vbcrlf)")
Next
txtstream.WriteLine("Response.Write(""</tr>"" & vbcrlf)")
Next


Case "Single-Line Vertical"


Dim ob As Object = objs.ItemIndex(0)


For Each prop In ob.Properties_
txtstream.WriteLine("Response.Write(""<tr><th>"     +     prop.Name     +
"</th><td>" + GetValue(prop.Name, ob) + "</td></tr>"" & vbcrlf)")
Next


Case "Multi-Line Vertical"


Dim ob As Object = objs.ItemIndex(0)
For Each prop In ob.Properties_
txtstream.WriteLine("Response.Write(""<tr><th>" + prop.Name + "</th>"" &
vbcrlf)")
For Each obj As Object In objs
txtstream.WriteLine("Response.Write(""<td>"  +  GetValue(prop.name, obj)  +
"</td>"" & vbcrlf)")
Next
txtstream.WriteLine("Response.Write(""</tr>"" & vbcrlf)")
Next
```

```
End Select



txtstream.WriteLine("Response.Write(""</table>"" & vbcrlf)")
txtstream.WriteLine("%>")
txtstream.WriteLine("</body>")
txtstream.WriteLine("</html>")
txtstream.Close()


End Sub
```

CREATE HTA CODE

Inside this sub routine is the code to create an HTA Application. You simply pass in the collection generated by the Return_Management_Collection and specify its orientation.

```
Public Sub Create_HTA_Code(ByVal objs As SWbemObjectSet, ByVal Orientation As String)


    txtstream         =         fso.OpenTextFile(Application.StartupPath         +
"\\Win32_Process.hta", 2, True, -2)
    txtstream.WriteLine("<html>")
    txtstream.WriteLine("<head>")
    txtstream.WriteLine("<HTA:APPLICATION ")
    txtstream.WriteLine("ID = ""Process"" ")
    txtstream.WriteLine("APPLICATIONNAME = ""Process"" ")
    txtstream.WriteLine("SCROLL = ""yes"" ")
    txtstream.WriteLine("SINGLEINSTANCE = ""yes"" ")
    txtstream.WriteLine("WINDOWSTATE = ""maximize"" >")
    txtstream.WriteLine("<title>Win32_Process</title>")
    txtstream.WriteLine("<style type='text/css'>")
    txtstream.WriteLine("body")
    txtstream.WriteLine("{")
    txtstream.WriteLine("   PADDING-RIGHT: 0px;")
    txtstream.WriteLine("   PADDING-LEFT: 0px;")
    txtstream.WriteLine("   PADDING-BOTTOM: 0px;")
    txtstream.WriteLine("   MARGIN: 0px;")
    txtstream.WriteLine("   COLOR: #333;")
```

```
txtstream.WriteLine("   PADDING-TOP: opx;")
txtstream.WriteLine("   FONT-FAMILY: verdana, arial, helvetica, sans-serif;")
txtstream.WriteLine("}")
txtstream.WriteLine("table")
txtstream.WriteLine("{")
txtstream.WriteLine("   BORDER-RIGHT: #999999 1px solid;")
txtstream.WriteLine("   PADDING-RIGHT: 1px;")
txtstream.WriteLine("   PADDING-LEFT: 1px;")
txtstream.WriteLine("   PADDING-BOTTOM: 1px;")
txtstream.WriteLine("   LINE-HEIGHT: 8px;")
txtstream.WriteLine("   PADDING-TOP: 1px;")
txtstream.WriteLine("   BORDER-BOTTOM: #999 1px solid;")
txtstream.WriteLine("   BACKGROUND-COLOR: #eeeeee;")
txtstream.WriteLine("
filter:progid:DXImageTransform.Microsoft.Shadow(color='silver',    Direction=135,
Strength=16)")
txtstream.WriteLine("}")
txtstream.WriteLine("th")
txtstream.WriteLine("{")
txtstream.WriteLine("   BORDER-RIGHT: #999999 3px solid;")
txtstream.WriteLine("   PADDING-RIGHT: 6px;")
txtstream.WriteLine("   PADDING-LEFT: 6px;")
txtstream.WriteLine("   FONT-WEIGHT: Bold;")
txtstream.WriteLine("   FONT-SIZE: 14px;")
txtstream.WriteLine("   PADDING-BOTTOM: 6px;")
txtstream.WriteLine("   COLOR: darkred;")
txtstream.WriteLine("   LINE-HEIGHT: 14px;")
txtstream.WriteLine("   PADDING-TOP: 6px;")
txtstream.WriteLine("   BORDER-BOTTOM: #999 1px solid;")
txtstream.WriteLine("   BACKGROUND-COLOR: #eeeeee;")
txtstream.WriteLine("   FONT-FAMILY: font-family: Cambria, serif;")
txtstream.WriteLine("   FONT-SIZE: 12px;")
txtstream.WriteLine("   text-align: left;")
```

```
txtstream.WriteLine("    white-Space: nowrap;")
txtstream.WriteLine("}")
txtstream.WriteLine(".th")
txtstream.WriteLine("{")
txtstream.WriteLine("    BORDER-RIGHT: #999999 2px solid;")
txtstream.WriteLine("    PADDING-RIGHT: 6px;")
txtstream.WriteLine("    PADDING-LEFT: 6px;")
txtstream.WriteLine("    FONT-WEIGHT: Bold;")
txtstream.WriteLine("    PADDING-BOTTOM: 6px;")
txtstream.WriteLine("    COLOR: black;")
txtstream.WriteLine("    PADDING-TOP: 6px;")
txtstream.WriteLine("    BORDER-BOTTOM: #999 2px solid;")
txtstream.WriteLine("    BACKGROUND-COLOR: #eeeeee;")
txtstream.WriteLine("    FONT-FAMILY: font-family: Cambria, serif;")
txtstream.WriteLine("    FONT-SIZE: 10px;")
txtstream.WriteLine("    text-align: right;")
txtstream.WriteLine("    white-Space: nowrap;")
txtstream.WriteLine("}")
txtstream.WriteLine("td")
txtstream.WriteLine("{")
txtstream.WriteLine("    BORDER-RIGHT: #999999 3px solid;")
txtstream.WriteLine("    PADDING-RIGHT: 6px;")
txtstream.WriteLine("    PADDING-LEFT: 6px;")
txtstream.WriteLine("    FONT-WEIGHT: Normal;")
txtstream.WriteLine("    PADDING-BOTTOM: 6px;")
txtstream.WriteLine("    COLOR: navy;")
txtstream.WriteLine("    LINE-HEIGHT: 14px;")
txtstream.WriteLine("    PADDING-TOP: 6px;")
txtstream.WriteLine("    BORDER-BOTTOM: #999 1px solid;")
txtstream.WriteLine("    BACKGROUND-COLOR: #eeeeee;")
txtstream.WriteLine("    FONT-FAMILY: font-family: Cambria, serif;")
txtstream.WriteLine("    FONT-SIZE: 12px;")
txtstream.WriteLine("    text-align: left;")
```

```
txtstream.WriteLine("    white-Space: nowrap;")
txtstream.WriteLine("}")
txtstream.WriteLine("div")
txtstream.WriteLine("{")
txtstream.WriteLine("    BORDER-RIGHT: #999999 3px solid;")
txtstream.WriteLine("    PADDING-RIGHT: 6px;")
txtstream.WriteLine("    PADDING-LEFT: 6px;")
txtstream.WriteLine("    FONT-WEIGHT: Normal;")
txtstream.WriteLine("    PADDING-BOTTOM: 6px;")
txtstream.WriteLine("    COLOR: white;")
txtstream.WriteLine("    PADDING-TOP: 6px;")
txtstream.WriteLine("    BORDER-BOTTOM: #999 1px solid;")
txtstream.WriteLine("    BACKGROUND-COLOR: navy;")
txtstream.WriteLine("    FONT-FAMILY: font-family: Cambria, serif;")
txtstream.WriteLine("    FONT-SIZE: 10px;")
txtstream.WriteLine("    text-align: left;")
txtstream.WriteLine("    white-Space: nowrap;")
txtstream.WriteLine("}")
txtstream.WriteLine("span")
txtstream.WriteLine("{")
txtstream.WriteLine("    BORDER-RIGHT: #999999 3px solid;")
txtstream.WriteLine("    PADDING-RIGHT: 3px;")
txtstream.WriteLine("    PADDING-LEFT: 3px;")
txtstream.WriteLine("    FONT-WEIGHT: Normal;")
txtstream.WriteLine("    PADDING-BOTTOM: 3px;")
txtstream.WriteLine("    COLOR: white;")
txtstream.WriteLine("    PADDING-TOP: 3px;")
txtstream.WriteLine("    BORDER-BOTTOM: #999 1px solid;")
txtstream.WriteLine("    BACKGROUND-COLOR: navy;")
txtstream.WriteLine("    FONT-FAMILY: font-family: Cambria, serif;")
txtstream.WriteLine("    FONT-SIZE: 10px;")
txtstream.WriteLine("    text-align: left;")
txtstream.WriteLine("    white-Space: nowrap;")
```

```
txtstream.WriteLine("    display: inline-block;")
txtstream.WriteLine("    width: 100%;")
txtstream.WriteLine("}")
txtstream.WriteLine("textarea")
txtstream.WriteLine("{")
txtstream.WriteLine("    BORDER-RIGHT: #999999 3px solid;")
txtstream.WriteLine("    PADDING-RIGHT: 3px;")
txtstream.WriteLine("    PADDING-LEFT: 3px;")
txtstream.WriteLine("    FONT-WEIGHT: Normal;")
txtstream.WriteLine("    PADDING-BOTTOM: 3px;")
txtstream.WriteLine("    COLOR: white;")
txtstream.WriteLine("    PADDING-TOP: 3px;")
txtstream.WriteLine("    BORDER-BOTTOM: #999 1px solid;")
txtstream.WriteLine("    BACKGROUND-COLOR: navy;")
txtstream.WriteLine("    FONT-FAMILY: font-family: Cambria, serif;")
txtstream.WriteLine("    FONT-SIZE: 10px;")
txtstream.WriteLine("    text-align: left;")
txtstream.WriteLine("    white-Space: nowrap;")
txtstream.WriteLine("    width: 100%;")
txtstream.WriteLine("}")
txtstream.WriteLine("select")
txtstream.WriteLine("{")
txtstream.WriteLine("    BORDER-RIGHT: #999999 3px solid;")
txtstream.WriteLine("    PADDING-RIGHT: 6px;")
txtstream.WriteLine("    PADDING-LEFT: 6px;")
txtstream.WriteLine("    FONT-WEIGHT: Normal;")
txtstream.WriteLine("    PADDING-BOTTOM: 6px;")
txtstream.WriteLine("    COLOR: white;")
txtstream.WriteLine("    PADDING-TOP: 6px;")
txtstream.WriteLine("    BORDER-BOTTOM: #999 1px solid;")
txtstream.WriteLine("    BACKGROUND-COLOR: navy;")
txtstream.WriteLine("    FONT-FAMILY: font-family: Cambria, serif;")
txtstream.WriteLine("    FONT-SIZE: 10px;")
```

```
txtstream.WriteLine("    text-align: left;")
txtstream.WriteLine("    white-Space: nowrap;")
txtstream.WriteLine("    width: 100%;")
txtstream.WriteLine("}")
txtstream.WriteLine("input")
txtstream.WriteLine("{")
txtstream.WriteLine("    BORDER-RIGHT: #999999 3px solid;")
txtstream.WriteLine("    PADDING-RIGHT: 3px;")
txtstream.WriteLine("    PADDING-LEFT: 3px;")
txtstream.WriteLine("    FONT-WEIGHT: Bold;")
txtstream.WriteLine("    PADDING-BOTTOM: 3px;")
txtstream.WriteLine("    COLOR: white;")
txtstream.WriteLine("    PADDING-TOP: 3px;")
txtstream.WriteLine("    BORDER-BOTTOM: #999 1px solid;")
txtstream.WriteLine("    BACKGROUND-COLOR: navy;")
txtstream.WriteLine("    FONT-FAMILY: font-family: Cambria, serif;")
txtstream.WriteLine("    FONT-SIZE: 12px;")
txtstream.WriteLine("    text-align: left;")
txtstream.WriteLine("    display: table-cell;")
txtstream.WriteLine("    white-Space: nowrap;")
txtstream.WriteLine("    width: 100%;")
txtstream.WriteLine("}")
txtstream.WriteLine("h1 {")
txtstream.WriteLine("color: antiquewhite;")
txtstream.WriteLine("text-shadow: 1px 1px 1px black;")
txtstream.WriteLine("padding: 3px;")
txtstream.WriteLine("text-align: center;")
txtstream.WriteLine("box-shadow: inset 2px 2px 5px rgba(0,0,0,0.5), inset -2px -2px 5px rgba(255,255,255,0.5)")
txtstream.WriteLine("}")
txtstream.WriteLine("</style>")
txtstream.WriteLine("</head>")
txtstream.WriteLine("<body>")
```

```
txtstream.WriteLine("<table Border='1' cellpadding='1' cellspacing='1'>")

Select Case Orientation


Case "Single-Line Horizontal"

Dim ob As Object = objs.ItemIndex(0)
txtstream.WriteLine("<tr>")
For Each prop In ob.Properties_
txtstream.WriteLine("<th>" + prop.Name + "</th>")
Next
txtstream.WriteLine("</tr>")
txtstream.WriteLine("<tr>")
For Each prop As Object In ob.Properties_
Dim value As String = GetValue(prop.Name, ob)
txtstream.WriteLine("<td>" + value + "</td>")
Next
txtstream.WriteLine("</tr>")


Case "Multi-Line Horizontal"

Dim ob As Object = objs.ItemIndex(0)
txtstream.WriteLine("<tr>")
For Each prop In ob.Properties_
txtstream.WriteLine("<th>" + prop.Name + "</th>")
Next
txtstream.WriteLine("</tr>")
For Each obj As Object In objs
txtstream.WriteLine("<tr>")
For Each prop As Object In obj.Properties_
Dim value As String = GetValue(prop.Name, obj)
```

```vb
        txtstream.WriteLine("<td>" + value + "</td>")
    Next
        txtstream.WriteLine("</tr>")
    Next


    Case "Single-Line Vertical"


        Dim ob As Object = objs.ItemIndex(0)

        For Each prop In ob.Properties_
        txtstream.WriteLine("<tr><th>"    +    prop.Name    +    "</th><td>"    +
    GetValue(prop.Name, ob) + "</td></tr>")
        Next


    Case "Multi-Line Vertical"


        Dim ob As Object = objs.ItemIndex(0)
        For Each prop In ob.Properties_
        txtstream.WriteLine("<tr><th>" + prop.Name + "</th>")
        For Each obj As Object In objs
        txtstream.WriteLine("<td>" + GetValue(prop.name, obj) + "</td>")
        Next
        txtstream.WriteLine("</tr>")
        Next


    End Select


    txtstream.WriteLine("</table>")
```

```
txtstream.WriteLine("</body>")
txtstream.WriteLine("</html>")
txtstream.Close()

End Sub
```

CREATE HTML CODE

Inside this sub routine is the code to create an HTML Webpage that can be saved and displayed using the Web Browser control or saved and displayed at a later time.

You simply pass in the collection generated by the Return_Management_Collection and specify its orientation.

Public Sub Create_HTML_Code(ByVal objs As SWbemObjectSet, ByVal Orientation As String)

```
txtstream = fso.OpenTextFile(Application.StartupPath +
"\\Win32_Process.html", 2, True, -2)
txtstream.WriteLine("<html>")
txtstream.WriteLine("<head>")
txtstream.WriteLine("<title>Win32_Process</title>")
txtstream.WriteLine("<style type='text/css'>")
txtstream.WriteLine("body")
txtstream.WriteLine("{")
txtstream.WriteLine("    PADDING-RIGHT: 0px;")
txtstream.WriteLine("    PADDING-LEFT: 0px;")
txtstream.WriteLine("    PADDING-BOTTOM: 0px;")
txtstream.WriteLine("    MARGIN: 0px;")
txtstream.WriteLine("    COLOR: #333;")
txtstream.WriteLine("    PADDING-TOP: 0px;")
txtstream.WriteLine("    FONT-FAMILY: verdana, arial, helvetica, sans-serif;")
txtstream.WriteLine("}")
txtstream.WriteLine("table")
txtstream.WriteLine("{")
txtstream.WriteLine("    BORDER-RIGHT: #999999 1px solid;")
```

```
txtstream.WriteLine("    PADDING-RIGHT: 1px;")
txtstream.WriteLine("    PADDING-LEFT: 1px;")
txtstream.WriteLine("    PADDING-BOTTOM: 1px;")
txtstream.WriteLine("    LINE-HEIGHT: 8px;")
txtstream.WriteLine("    PADDING-TOP: 1px;")
txtstream.WriteLine("    BORDER-BOTTOM: #999 1px solid;")
txtstream.WriteLine("    BACKGROUND-COLOR: #eeeeee;")
txtstream.WriteLine("
filter:progid:DXImageTransform.Microsoft.Shadow(color='silver',    Direction=135,
Strength=16)")
txtstream.WriteLine("}")
txtstream.WriteLine("th")
txtstream.WriteLine("{")
txtstream.WriteLine("    BORDER-RIGHT: #999999 3px solid;")
txtstream.WriteLine("    PADDING-RIGHT: 6px;")
txtstream.WriteLine("    PADDING-LEFT: 6px;")
txtstream.WriteLine("    FONT-WEIGHT: Bold;")
txtstream.WriteLine("    FONT-SIZE: 14px;")
txtstream.WriteLine("    PADDING-BOTTOM: 6px;")
txtstream.WriteLine("    COLOR: darkred;")
txtstream.WriteLine("    LINE-HEIGHT: 14px;")
txtstream.WriteLine("    PADDING-TOP: 6px;")
txtstream.WriteLine("    BORDER-BOTTOM: #999 1px solid;")
txtstream.WriteLine("    BACKGROUND-COLOR: #eeeeee;")
txtstream.WriteLine("    FONT-FAMILY: font-family: Cambria, serif;")
txtstream.WriteLine("    FONT-SIZE: 12px;")
txtstream.WriteLine("    text-align: left;")
txtstream.WriteLine("    white-Space: nowrap;")
txtstream.WriteLine("}")
txtstream.WriteLine(".th")
txtstream.WriteLine("{")
txtstream.WriteLine("    BORDER-RIGHT: #999999 2px solid;")
txtstream.WriteLine("    PADDING-RIGHT: 6px;")
```

```
txtstream.WriteLine("    PADDING-LEFT: 6px;")
txtstream.WriteLine("    FONT-WEIGHT: Bold;")
txtstream.WriteLine("    PADDING-BOTTOM: 6px;")
txtstream.WriteLine("    COLOR: black;")
txtstream.WriteLine("    PADDING-TOP: 6px;")
txtstream.WriteLine("    BORDER-BOTTOM: #999 2px solid;")
txtstream.WriteLine("    BACKGROUND-COLOR: #eeeeee;")
txtstream.WriteLine("    FONT-FAMILY: font-family: Cambria, serif;")
txtstream.WriteLine("    FONT-SIZE: 10px;")
txtstream.WriteLine("    text-align: right;")
txtstream.WriteLine("    white-Space: nowrap;")
txtstream.WriteLine("}")
txtstream.WriteLine("td")
txtstream.WriteLine("{")
txtstream.WriteLine("    BORDER-RIGHT: #999999 3px solid;")
txtstream.WriteLine("    PADDING-RIGHT: 6px;")
txtstream.WriteLine("    PADDING-LEFT: 6px;")
txtstream.WriteLine("    FONT-WEIGHT: Normal;")
txtstream.WriteLine("    PADDING-BOTTOM: 6px;")
txtstream.WriteLine("    COLOR: navy;")
txtstream.WriteLine("    LINE-HEIGHT: 14px;")
txtstream.WriteLine("    PADDING-TOP: 6px;")
txtstream.WriteLine("    BORDER-BOTTOM: #999 1px solid;")
txtstream.WriteLine("    BACKGROUND-COLOR: #eeeeee;")
txtstream.WriteLine("    FONT-FAMILY: font-family: Cambria, serif;")
txtstream.WriteLine("    FONT-SIZE: 12px;")
txtstream.WriteLine("    text-align: left;")
txtstream.WriteLine("    white-Space: nowrap;")
txtstream.WriteLine("}")
txtstream.WriteLine("div")
txtstream.WriteLine("{")
txtstream.WriteLine("    BORDER-RIGHT: #999999 3px solid;")
txtstream.WriteLine("    PADDING-RIGHT: 6px;")
```

```
txtstream.WriteLine("   PADDING-LEFT: 6px;")
txtstream.WriteLine("   FONT-WEIGHT: Normal;")
txtstream.WriteLine("   PADDING-BOTTOM: 6px;")
txtstream.WriteLine("   COLOR: white;")
txtstream.WriteLine("   PADDING-TOP: 6px;")
txtstream.WriteLine("   BORDER-BOTTOM: #999 1px solid;")
txtstream.WriteLine("   BACKGROUND-COLOR: navy;")
txtstream.WriteLine("   FONT-FAMILY: font-family: Cambria, serif;")
txtstream.WriteLine("   FONT-SIZE: 10px;")
txtstream.WriteLine("   text-align: left;")
txtstream.WriteLine("   white-Space: nowrap;")
txtstream.WriteLine("}")
txtstream.WriteLine("span")
txtstream.WriteLine("{")
txtstream.WriteLine("   BORDER-RIGHT: #999999 3px solid;")
txtstream.WriteLine("   PADDING-RIGHT: 3px;")
txtstream.WriteLine("   PADDING-LEFT: 3px;")
txtstream.WriteLine("   FONT-WEIGHT: Normal;")
txtstream.WriteLine("   PADDING-BOTTOM: 3px;")
txtstream.WriteLine("   COLOR: white;")
txtstream.WriteLine("   PADDING-TOP: 3px;")
txtstream.WriteLine("   BORDER-BOTTOM: #999 1px solid;")
txtstream.WriteLine("   BACKGROUND-COLOR: navy;")
txtstream.WriteLine("   FONT-FAMILY: font-family: Cambria, serif;")
txtstream.WriteLine("   FONT-SIZE: 10px;")
txtstream.WriteLine("   text-align: left;")
txtstream.WriteLine("   white-Space: nowrap;")
txtstream.WriteLine("   display: inline-block;")
txtstream.WriteLine("   width: 100%;")
txtstream.WriteLine("}")
txtstream.WriteLine("textarea")
txtstream.WriteLine("{")
txtstream.WriteLine("   BORDER-RIGHT: #999999 3px solid;")
```

```
txtstream.WriteLine("    PADDING-RIGHT: 3px;")
txtstream.WriteLine("    PADDING-LEFT: 3px;")
txtstream.WriteLine("    FONT-WEIGHT: Normal;")
txtstream.WriteLine("    PADDING-BOTTOM: 3px;")
txtstream.WriteLine("    COLOR: white;")
txtstream.WriteLine("    PADDING-TOP: 3px;")
txtstream.WriteLine("    BORDER-BOTTOM: #999 1px solid;")
txtstream.WriteLine("    BACKGROUND-COLOR: navy;")
txtstream.WriteLine("    FONT-FAMILY: font-family: Cambria, serif;")
txtstream.WriteLine("    FONT-SIZE: 10px;")
txtstream.WriteLine("    text-align: left;")
txtstream.WriteLine("    white-Space: nowrap;")
txtstream.WriteLine("    width: 100%;")
txtstream.WriteLine("}")
txtstream.WriteLine("select")
txtstream.WriteLine("{")
txtstream.WriteLine("    BORDER-RIGHT: #999999 3px solid;")
txtstream.WriteLine("    PADDING-RIGHT: 6px;")
txtstream.WriteLine("    PADDING-LEFT: 6px;")
txtstream.WriteLine("    FONT-WEIGHT: Normal;")
txtstream.WriteLine("    PADDING-BOTTOM: 6px;")
txtstream.WriteLine("    COLOR: white;")
txtstream.WriteLine("    PADDING-TOP: 6px;")
txtstream.WriteLine("    BORDER-BOTTOM: #999 1px solid;")
txtstream.WriteLine("    BACKGROUND-COLOR: navy;")
txtstream.WriteLine("    FONT-FAMILY: font-family: Cambria, serif;")
txtstream.WriteLine("    FONT-SIZE: 10px;")
txtstream.WriteLine("    text-align: left;")
txtstream.WriteLine("    white-Space: nowrap;")
txtstream.WriteLine("    width: 100%;")
txtstream.WriteLine("}")
txtstream.WriteLine("input")
txtstream.WriteLine("{")
```

```
txtstream.WriteLine("   BORDER-RIGHT: #999999 3px solid;")
txtstream.WriteLine("   PADDING-RIGHT: 3px;")
txtstream.WriteLine("   PADDING-LEFT: 3px;")
txtstream.WriteLine("   FONT-WEIGHT: Bold;")
txtstream.WriteLine("   PADDING-BOTTOM: 3px;")
txtstream.WriteLine("   COLOR: white;")
txtstream.WriteLine("   PADDING-TOP: 3px;")
txtstream.WriteLine("   BORDER-BOTTOM: #999 1px solid;")
txtstream.WriteLine("   BACKGROUND-COLOR: navy;")
txtstream.WriteLine("   FONT-FAMILY: font-family: Cambria, serif;")
txtstream.WriteLine("   FONT-SIZE: 12px;")
txtstream.WriteLine("   text-align: left;")
txtstream.WriteLine("   display: table-cell;")
txtstream.WriteLine("   white-Space: nowrap;")
txtstream.WriteLine("   width: 100%;")
txtstream.WriteLine("}")
txtstream.WriteLine("h1 {")
txtstream.WriteLine("color: antiquewhite;")
txtstream.WriteLine("text-shadow: 1px 1px 1px black;")
txtstream.WriteLine("padding: 3px;")
txtstream.WriteLine("text-align: center;")
txtstream.WriteLine("box-shadow: inset 2px 2px 5px rgba(0,0,0,0.5), inset -2px -2px 5px rgba(255,255,255,0.5)")
txtstream.WriteLine("}")
txtstream.WriteLine("</style>")
txtstream.WriteLine("</head>")
txtstream.WriteLine("<body>")
txtstream.WriteLine("<table Border='1' cellpadding='1' cellspacing='1'>")

Select Case Orientation

Case "Single-Line Horizontal"
```

```
Dim ob As Object = objs.ItemIndex(0)
txtstream.WriteLine("<tr>")
For Each prop In ob.Properties_
txtstream.WriteLine("<th>" + prop.Name + "</th>")
Next
txtstream.WriteLine("</tr>")
txtstream.WriteLine("<tr>")
For Each prop As Object In ob.Properties_
Dim value As String = GetValue(prop.Name, ob)
txtstream.WriteLine("<td>" + value + "</td>")
Next
txtstream.WriteLine("</tr>")


Case "Multi-Line Horizontal"

Dim ob As Object = objs.ItemIndex(0)
txtstream.WriteLine("<tr>")
For Each prop In ob.Properties_
txtstream.WriteLine("<th>" + prop.Name + "</th>")
Next
txtstream.WriteLine("</tr>")
For Each obj As Object In objs
txtstream.WriteLine("<tr>")
For Each prop As Object In obj.Properties_
Dim value As String = GetValue(prop.Name, obj)
txtstream.WriteLine("<td>" + value + "</td>")
Next
txtstream.WriteLine("</tr>")
Next

Case "Single-Line Vertical"
```

```
Dim ob As Object = objs.ItemIndex(0)

For Each prop In ob.Properties_
txtstream.WriteLine("<tr><th>"    +    prop.Name    +    "</th><td>"    +
GetValue(prop.Name, ob) + "</td></tr>")
Next


Case "Multi-Line Vertical"


Dim ob As Object = objs.ItemIndex(0)
For Each prop In ob.Properties_
txtstream.WriteLine("<tr><th>" + prop.Name + "</th>")
For Each obj As Object In objs
txtstream.WriteLine("<td>" + GetValue(prop.name, obj) + "</td>")
Next
txtstream.WriteLine("</tr>")
Next


End Select

txtstream.WriteLine("</table>")
txtstream.WriteLine("</body>")
txtstream.WriteLine("</html>")
txtstream.Close()


End Sub
```

CREATE THE CSV FILE

Inside this sub routine is the code to create a CSV file. It is a separate routine because its extension -.csv – is seen by Excel – assuming it is installed as a text-based data file and knows what to do with it to display its contents.

You simply pass in the collection generated by the Return_Management_Collection and specify its orientation.

```
Public Sub Create_CSV_File_Code(ByVal objs As SWbemObjectSet, ByVal
Orientation As String)

txtstream          =          fso.OpenTextFile(Application.StartupPath          &
"\\Win32_Process.csv", 2, True, -2)

Dim tempstr As String = ""

Select Case Orientation

Case "Horizontal"

Dim ob As Object = objs.ItemIndex(0)
For Each prop As Object In ob.Properties_

If tempstr <> "" Then

tempstr = tempstr + ","

End If
tempstr = tempstr + prop.Name
```

```
Next
txtstream.WriteLine(tempstr)
tempstr = ""

For Each obj As Object In objs

For Each prop As Object In obj.Properties_

If tempstr <> "" Then

tempstr = tempstr + ","
End If

tempstr = tempstr + Chr(34) + GetValue(prop.Name, obj) + Chr(34)

Next

txtstream.WriteLine(tempstr)
tempstr = ""
Next

txtstream.Close()

Case "Vertical"

Dim ob As Object = objs.ItemIndex(0)

For Each prop As Object In ob.Properties_

tempstr = prop.Name

For Each obj As Object In objs
```

```
If tempstr <> "" Then

tempstr = tempstr + ","
End If

tempstr = tempstr + Chr(34) + GetValue(prop.Name, obj) + Chr(34)

Next

txtstream.WriteLine(tempstr)
tempstr = ""

Next


End Select


End Sub
```

CREATE THE EXCEL FILE

Inside this sub routine is the code to create a CSV file and then open it using an older version of Excel.

```
Public Sub Create_Excel_File_Code(ByVal objs As SWbemObjectSet, ByVal Orientation As String)

txtstream = fso.OpenTextFile(Application.StartupPath & "\\Win32_Process.csv", 2, True, -2)

Dim tempstr As String = ""

Select Case Orientation

Case "Horizontal"

Dim ob As Object = objs.ItemIndex(0)
For Each prop As Object In ob.Properties_

If tempstr <> "" Then

tempstr = tempstr + ","

End If
tempstr = tempstr + prop.Name
```

```
Next
txtstream.WriteLine(tempstr)
tempstr = ""

For Each obj As Object In objs

For Each prop As Object In obj.Properties_

If tempstr <> "" Then

tempstr = tempstr + ","
End If

tempstr = tempstr + Chr(34) + GetValue(prop.Name, obj) + Chr(34)

Next

txtstream.WriteLine(tempstr)
tempstr = ""
Next

txtstream.Close()

Case "Vertical"

Dim ob As Object = objs.ItemIndex(0)

For Each prop As Object In ob.Properties_

tempstr = prop.Name

For Each obj As Object In objs
```

```
If tempstr <> "" Then

tempstr = tempstr + ","
End If

tempstr = tempstr + Chr(34) + GetValue(prop.Name, obj) + Chr(34)

Next

txtstream.WriteLine(tempstr)
tempstr = ""

Next


End Select

Dim ws As Object = CreateObject("Wscript.Shell")
ws.Run(Application.StartupPath & "\\Win32_Process.csv")


End Sub
```

EXCEL AUTOMATION CODE

Inside this sub routine is the code to create an instance of Excel and populate a worksheet. Both horizontal and vertical orientations are available, and the code automatically aligns and autofits the cells.

```
Public      Sub      Create_Excel_Automation_File_Code(ByVal      objs      As
SWbemObjectSet, ByVal Orientation As String)

Dim oexcel As Object = CreateObject("Excel.Applicaiton")
Dim wb As Object = oexcel.WorkBooks.Add()
Dim ws As Object = wb.Worksheets(1)
ws.Name = "Win32_Process"
Dim x As Integer = 1
Dim y As Integer = 2
Dim ob As Object = objs.ItemIndex(0)

Select Case Orientation

Case "Horizontal"

For Each prop As Object In ob.Properties_
ws.Cells(1, x) = prop.Name
x = x + 1
Next
x = 1
```

```vb
For Each obj As Object In objs

    For Each prop As Object In obj.Properties_
    ws.Cells(y, x) = GetValue(prop.Name, obj)
    x = x + 1
    Next
    x = 1
    y = y + 1
Next

Case "Vertical"

    For Each prop As Object In ob.Properties_
    ws.Cells(x, 1) = prop.Name
    x = x + 1
    Next
    x = 1
    For Each obj As Object In objs

    For Each prop As Object In obj.Properties_
    ws.Cells(x, y) = GetValue(prop.Name, obj)
    x = x + 1
    Next
    x = 1
    y = y + 1
    Next

End Select

ws.Columns.HorizontalAlignment = -3141
ws.Columns.AutoFit()

End Sub
```

CREATE CUSTOM DELIMITED TEXT FILE

This sub routine is designed to provide you with maximum flexibility. You choose the orientation and the delimiter.

```
Public Sub Create_Text_File_Code(ByVal objs As SWbemObjectSet, ByVal Orientation As String, ByVal Delim As String)


txtstream = fso.OpenTextFile(Application.StartupPath & "\\Win32_Process.txt", 2, True, -2)
Dim tempstr As String = ""

Select Case Orientation

Case "Horizontal"

Dim ob As Object = objs.ItemIndex(0)
For Each prop As Object In ob.Properties_

If tempstr <> "" Then

tempstr = tempstr + Delim

End If
tempstr = tempstr + prop.Name
```

```vb
Next
txtstream.WriteLine(tempstr)
tempstr = ""

For Each obj As Object In objs

For Each prop As Object In obj.Properties_

If tempstr <> "" Then

tempstr = tempstr + Delim
End If

tempstr = tempstr + Chr(34) + GetValue(prop.Name, obj) + Chr(34)

Next

txtstream.WriteLine(tempstr)
tempstr = ""
Next

txtstream.Close()

Case "Vertical"

Dim ob As Object = objs.ItemIndex(0)

For Each prop As Object In ob.Properties_

tempstr = prop.Name

For Each obj As Object In objs
```

```
If tempstr <> "" Then

tempstr = tempstr + Delim
End If

tempstr = tempstr + Chr(34) + GetValue(prop.Name, obj) + Chr(34)

Next

txtstream.WriteLine(tempstr)
tempstr = ""

Next


End Select


End Sub
```

CREATE AN EXCEL

SPREADSHEET TEXT FILE

Simply put, this routine creates an Excel Spreadsheet File that will automatically be displayed by Excel as a worksheet.

```
Public Sub Create_Excel_SpreadSheet(ByVal objs As SWbemObjectSet)


Dim ws As Object = CreateObject("WScript.Shell")


txtstream = fso.OpenTextFile(Application.StartupPath + "\\ProcessExcel.xml",
2, True, -2)
    txtstream.WriteLine("<?xml version='1.0'?>")
    txtstream.WriteLine("<?mso-application progid='Excel.Sheet'?>")
    txtstream.WriteLine("<Workbook            xmlns='urn:schemas-microsoft-
com:office:spreadsheet'          xmlns:o='urn:schemas-microsoft-com:office:office'
xmlns:x='urn:schemas-microsoft-com:office:excel'          xmlns:ss='urn:schemas-
microsoft-com:office:spreadsheet'          xmlns:html='http://www.w3.org/TR/REC-
html40'>")
    txtstream.WriteLine("        <Documentproperties       xmlns='urn:schemas-
microsoft-com:office:office'>")
    txtstream.WriteLine("               <Author>Windows User</Author>")
    txtstream.WriteLine("               <LastAuthor>Windows
User</LastAuthor>")
    txtstream.WriteLine("               <Created>2007-11-
27T19:36:16Z</Created>")
```

```
txtstream.WriteLine("                    <Version>12.00</Version>")
txtstream.WriteLine("          </Documentproperties>")
txtstream.WriteLine("        <ExcelWorkbook              xmlns='urn:schemas-
microsoft-com:office:excel'>")
txtstream.WriteLine("
    <WindowHeight>11835</WindowHeight>")
txtstream.WriteLine("
    <WindowWidth>18960</WindowWidth>")
txtstream.WriteLine("                    <WindowTopX>120</WindowTopX>")
txtstream.WriteLine("                    <WindowTopY>135</WindowTopY>")
txtstream.WriteLine("
    <ProtectStructure>False</ProtectStructure>")
txtstream.WriteLine("
    <ProtectWindows>False</ProtectWindows>")
txtstream.WriteLine("          </ExcelWorkbook>")
txtstream.WriteLine("        <Styles>")
txtstream.WriteLine("                    <Style              ss:ID='Default'
ss:Name='Normal'>")
txtstream.WriteLine("                        <Alignment
ss:Vertical='Bottom'/>")
txtstream.WriteLine("                        <Borders/>")
txtstream.WriteLine("                        <Font    ss:FontName='Calibri'
x:Family='Swiss' ss:Size='11' ss:Color='#000000'/>")
txtstream.WriteLine("                        <Interior/>")
txtstream.WriteLine("                        <NumberFormat/>")
txtstream.WriteLine("                        <Protection/>")
txtstream.WriteLine("          </Style>")
txtstream.WriteLine("          <Style ss:ID='s62'>")
txtstream.WriteLine("                        <Borders/>")
txtstream.WriteLine("                        <Font    ss:FontName='Calibri'
x:Family='Swiss' ss:Size='11' ss:Color='#000000' ss:Bold='1'/>")
txtstream.WriteLine("          </Style>")
txtstream.WriteLine("          <Style ss:ID='s63'>")
```

```vb
        txtstream.WriteLine("                              <Alignment
ss:Horizontal='Left' ss:Vertical='Bottom' ss:Indent='2'/>")
        txtstream.WriteLine("                                <Font  ss:FontName='Verdana'
x:Family='Swiss' ss:Size='7.7' ss:Color='#000000'/>")
        txtstream.WriteLine("                      </Style>")
        txtstream.WriteLine("    </Styles>")
        txtstream.WriteLine("<Worksheet ss:Name='Process'>")
        txtstream.WriteLine("                <Table    x:FullColumns='1'    x:FullRows='1'
ss:DefaultRowHeight='24.9375'>")
        txtstream.WriteLine("                <Column ss:AutoFitWidth='1'  ss:Width='82.5'
ss:Span='5'/>")
        Dim ob As Object = objs.ItemIndex(0)
        txtstream.WriteLine("    <Row ss:AutoFitHeight='0'>")
        For Each prop In ob.Properties_
        txtstream.WriteLine("        <Cell ss:StyleID='s62'><Data ss:Type='String'>" +
prop.Name + "</Data></Cell>")
        Next
        txtstream.WriteLine("    </Row>")
        For Each obj As Object In objs
        txtstream.WriteLine("    <Row ss:AutoFitHeight='0' ss:Height='13.5'>")
        For Each prop As Object In obj.Properties_
        txtstream.WriteLine("            <Cell><Data ss:Type='String'><![CDATA[" +
GetValue(prop.Name, obj) + "]]></Data></Cell>")
        Next
        txtstream.WriteLine("    </Row>")
        Next
        txtstream.WriteLine("    </Table>")
        txtstream.WriteLine("          <WorksheetOptions          xmlns='urn:schemas-
microsoft-com:office:excel'>")
        txtstream.WriteLine("                 <PageSetup>")
        txtstream.WriteLine("                      <Header x:Margin='0.3'/>")
        txtstream.WriteLine("                      <Footer x:Margin='0.3'/>")
```

```
txtstream.WriteLine("                              <PageMargins x:Bottom='0.75'
x:Left='0.7' x:Right='0.7' x:Top='0.75'/>")
txtstream.WriteLine("                    </PageSetup>")
txtstream.WriteLine("                    <Unsynced/>")
txtstream.WriteLine("                    <Print>")
txtstream.WriteLine("                        <FitHeight>0</FitHeight>")
txtstream.WriteLine("                        <ValidPrinterInfo/>")
txtstream.WriteLine("
    <HorizontalResolution>600</HorizontalResolution>")
txtstream.WriteLine("
    <VerticalResolution>600</VerticalResolution>")
txtstream.WriteLine("                    </Print>")
txtstream.WriteLine("                    <Selected/>")
txtstream.WriteLine("                    <Panes>")
txtstream.WriteLine("                        <Pane>")
txtstream.WriteLine("
    <Number>3</Number>")
txtstream.WriteLine("
    <ActiveRow>9</ActiveRow>")
txtstream.WriteLine("
    <ActiveCol>7</ActiveCol>")
txtstream.WriteLine("                        </Pane>")
txtstream.WriteLine("                    </Panes>")
txtstream.WriteLine("
    <ProtectObjects>False</ProtectObjects>")
txtstream.WriteLine("
    <ProtectScenarios>False</ProtectScenarios>")
txtstream.WriteLine("           </WorksheetOptions>")
txtstream.WriteLine("</Worksheet>")
txtstream.WriteLine("</Workbook>")
txtstream.Close()

ws.Run(Application.StartupPath & "\ProcessExcel.xml")
```

```
End Sub
```

CREATE AN XML FILE

This sub routine creates a very simple Element XML File. This file can be used with the MSDAOSP and therefore, becomes as database text file.

```
Public Sub Create_Element_XML_File_Code(ByVal objs As SWbemObjectSet)

txtstream           =            fso.OpenTextFile(Application.StartupPath            +
"\\Win32_Process.xml", 2, True, -2)
txtstream.WriteLine("<?xml version='1.0' encoding='iso-8859-1'?>")
txtstream.WriteLine("<data>")
For Each obj As Object In objs
txtstream.WriteLine("<Win32_process>")
For Each prop As Object In obj.Properties_

txtstream.WriteLine("<" + prop.Name + ">" + GetValue(prop.Name, obj) +
"</" + prop.Name + ">")
Next
txtstream.WriteLine("</Win32_process>")
Next
txtstream.WriteLine("</data>")
txtstream.Close()

End Sub
```

CREATE AN XML FOR XSL FILE

This sub routine creates a very simple Element XML File but is dependent upon the specified XSL file. This file cannot be used with the MSDAOSP due to its dependency on the XSL file.

```
Public    Sub    Create_Element_XML_For_XSL_Files_Code(ByVal    objs    As
SWbemObjectSet)

txtstream         =         fso.OpenTextFile(Application.StartupPath        +
"\\Win32_Process.xml", 2, True, -2)
    txtstream.WriteLine("<?xml version='1.0' encoding='iso-8859-1'?>")
    txtstream.WriteLine("<?xml-stylesheet        type='Text/xsl'        href='"    +
Application.StartupPath + "\\Win32_Process.xsl'?>")
    txtstream.WriteLine("<data>")
    For Each obj As Object In objs
    txtstream.WriteLine("<Win32_process>")
    For Each prop As Object In obj.Properties_

    txtstream.WriteLine("<" + prop.Name + ">" + GetValue(prop.Name, obj) +
"</" + prop.Name + ">")
    Next
    txtstream.WriteLine("</Win32_process>")
    Next
    txtstream.WriteLine("</data>")
    txtstream.Close()

End Sub
```

CREATE A SCHEMA XML

This sub routine creates a very simple Element XML File but is dependent upon the specified XSL file. It is opened by ADO and uses the MSDAOSP provider.

This file is then saved and can be used by the MSPERSIST provider.

```
Public Sub Create_Schema_XML_Files_Code(ByVal objs As SWbemObjectSet)

txtstream            =            fso.OpenTextFile(Application.StartupPath            +
"\\Win32_Process.xml", 2, True, -2)
txtstream.WriteLine("<?xml version='1.0' encoding='iso-8859-1'?>")
txtstream.WriteLine("<data>")
For Each obj As Object In objs
txtstream.WriteLine("<Win32_process>")
For Each prop As Object In obj.Properties_

txtstream.WriteLine("<" + prop.Name + ">" + GetValue(prop.Name, obj) +
"</" + prop.Name + ">")
Next
txtstream.WriteLine("</Win32_process>")
Next
txtstream.WriteLine("</data>")
txtstream.Close()

Dim rs1 As Object = CreateObject("ADODB.Recordset")
rs1.ActiveConnection            =            "Provider=MSDAOSP;            Data
Source=msxml2.DSOControl"
rs1.Open(Application.StartupPath & "\\Win32_Process.xml")
```

```
        If fso.FileExists(Application.StartupPath & "\\Win32_Process_Schema.xml") =
True Then

        fso.DeleteFile(Application.StartupPath + "\\Win32_Process_Schema.xml")
        End If

        rs1.Save(Application.StartupPath & "\\Win32_Process_Schema.xml", 1)



        End Sub
```

CREATE THE XSL FILES

Inside this sub routine is the code to create the XSL File designed to render the XML as an HTML Webpage. It can be saved and displayed using the Web Browser control or saved and displayed at a later time. Simply pass in the collection generated by the Return_Management_Collection and specify its orientation.

```
Public Sub Create_XSL_Files_Code(ByVal objs As SWbemObjectSet, ByVal Orientation As String)

Dim obj As Object = objs(0)

Select Case Orientation

Case "SINGLE LINE HORIZONTAL"

txtstream.WriteLine("<?xml version='1.0' encoding='UTF-8'?>")
txtstream.WriteLine("<xsl:stylesheet                    version='1.0' xmlns:xsl='http://www.w3.org/1999/XSL/Transform'>")
txtstream.WriteLine("<xsl:template match=""""/""""">")
txtstream.WriteLine("<html>")
txtstream.WriteLine("<head>")
txtstream.WriteLine("<title>Products</title>")
txtstream.WriteLine("<style type='text/css'>")
txtstream.WriteLine("th")
txtstream.WriteLine("{")
txtstream.WriteLine("    COLOR: darkred;")
```

```
txtstream.WriteLine("    BACKGROUND-COLOR: white;")
txtstream.WriteLine("    FONT-FAMILY:font-family: Cambria, serif;")
txtstream.WriteLine("    FONT-SIZE: 12px;")
txtstream.WriteLine("    text-align: left;")
txtstream.WriteLine("    white-Space: nowrap;")
txtstream.WriteLine("}")
txtstream.WriteLine("td")
txtstream.WriteLine("{")
txtstream.WriteLine("    COLOR: navy;")
txtstream.WriteLine("    BACKGROUND-COLOR: white;")
txtstream.WriteLine("    FONT-FAMILY: font-family: Cambria, serif;")
txtstream.WriteLine("    FONT-SIZE: 12px;")
txtstream.WriteLine("    text-align: left;")
txtstream.WriteLine("    white-Space: nowrap;")
txtstream.WriteLine("}")
txtstream.WriteLine("</style>")
txtstream.WriteLine("</head>")
txtstream.WriteLine("<body bgcolor='#333333'>")
txtstream.WriteLine("<table colspacing='3' colpadding='3'>")
txtstream.WriteLine("<tr>")
For Each prop As Object In obj.Properties_
txtstream.WriteLine("<th>" + prop.Name + "</th>")
Next
txtstream.WriteLine("</tr>")
txtstream.WriteLine("<tr>")
For Each prop As Object In obj.Properties_
txtstream.WriteLine("<td><xsl:value-of    select=""data/Win32_Process/"    &
prop.Name & """/></td>")
Next
txtstream.WriteLine("</tr>")
txtstream.WriteLine("</table>")
txtstream.WriteLine("</body>")
txtstream.WriteLine("</html>")
```

```
txtstream.WriteLine("</xsl:template>")
txtstream.WriteLine("</xsl:stylesheet>")
txtstream.Close()


Case "Multi Line Horizontal"


txtstream.WriteLine("<?xml version='1.0' encoding='UTF-8'?>")
txtstream.WriteLine("<xsl:stylesheet                              version='1.0'
xmlns:xsl='http://www.w3.org/1999/XSL/Transform'>")
txtstream.WriteLine("<xsl:template match=""/"">")
txtstream.WriteLine("<html>")
txtstream.WriteLine("<head>")
txtstream.WriteLine("<title>Products</title>")
txtstream.WriteLine("<style type='text/css'>")
txtstream.WriteLine("th")
txtstream.WriteLine("{")
txtstream.WriteLine("    COLOR: darkred;")
txtstream.WriteLine("    BACKGROUND-COLOR: white;")
txtstream.WriteLine("    FONT-FAMILY:font-family: Cambria, serif;")
txtstream.WriteLine("    FONT-SIZE: 12px;")
txtstream.WriteLine("    text-align: left;")
txtstream.WriteLine("    white-Space: nowrap;")
txtstream.WriteLine("}")
txtstream.WriteLine("td")
txtstream.WriteLine("{")
txtstream.WriteLine("    COLOR: navy;")
txtstream.WriteLine("    BACKGROUND-COLOR: white;")
txtstream.WriteLine("    FONT-FAMILY: font-family: Cambria, serif;")
txtstream.WriteLine("    FONT-SIZE: 12px;")
txtstream.WriteLine("    text-align: left;")
txtstream.WriteLine("    white-Space: nowrap;")
```

```vb
txtstream.WriteLine("}")
txtstream.WriteLine("</style>")
txtstream.WriteLine("</head>")
txtstream.WriteLine("<body bgcolor='#333333'>")
txtstream.WriteLine("<table colspacing='3' colpadding='3'>")
txtstream.WriteLine("<tr>")
For Each prop As Object In obj.Properties_
txtstream.WriteLine("<th>" + prop.Name + "</th>")
Next
txtstream.WriteLine("</tr>")
txtstream.WriteLine("<xsl:for-each select=""""data/Win32_Process"""">")
txtstream.WriteLine("<tr>")
For Each prop As Object In obj.Properties_
txtstream.WriteLine("<td><xsl:value-of    select="""""    +    prop.Name    +
""""/></td>")
Next
txtstream.WriteLine("</tr>")
txtstream.WriteLine("</xsl:for-each>")
txtstream.WriteLine("</table>")
txtstream.WriteLine("</body>")
txtstream.WriteLine("</html>")
txtstream.WriteLine("</xsl:template>")
txtstream.WriteLine("</xsl:stylesheet>")
txtstream.Close()


Case "Single Line Vertical"

txtstream.WriteLine("<?xml version='1.0' encoding='UTF-8'?>")
txtstream.WriteLine("<xsl:stylesheet                          version='1.0'
xmlns:xsl='http://www.w3.org/1999/XSL/Transform'>")
txtstream.WriteLine("<xsl:template match=""""/"""">")
txtstream.WriteLine("<html>")
```

```
txtstream.WriteLine("<head>")
txtstream.WriteLine("<title>Products</title>")
txtstream.WriteLine("<style type='text/css'>")
txtstream.WriteLine("th")
txtstream.WriteLine("{")
txtstream.WriteLine("    COLOR: darkred;")
txtstream.WriteLine("    BACKGROUND-COLOR: white;")
txtstream.WriteLine("    FONT-FAMILY:font-family: Cambria, serif;")
txtstream.WriteLine("    FONT-SIZE: 12px;")
txtstream.WriteLine("    text-align: left;")
txtstream.WriteLine("    white-Space: nowrap;")
txtstream.WriteLine("}")
txtstream.WriteLine("td")
txtstream.WriteLine("{")
txtstream.WriteLine("    COLOR: navy;")
txtstream.WriteLine("    BACKGROUND-COLOR: white;")
txtstream.WriteLine("    FONT-FAMILY: font-family: Cambria, serif;")
txtstream.WriteLine("    FONT-SIZE: 12px;")
txtstream.WriteLine("    text-align: left;")
txtstream.WriteLine("    white-Space: nowrap;")
txtstream.WriteLine("}")
txtstream.WriteLine("</style>")
txtstream.WriteLine("</head>")
txtstream.WriteLine("<body bgcolor='#333333'>")
txtstream.WriteLine("<table colspacing='3' colpadding='3'>")
For Each prop As Object In obj.Properties_
txtstream.WriteLine("<tr><th>" + prop.Name + "</th>")
txtstream.WriteLine("<td><xsl:value-of    select=""data/Win32_Process/"    +
prop.Name + """/></td></tr>")
Next
txtstream.WriteLine("</table>")
txtstream.WriteLine("</body>")
txtstream.WriteLine("</html>")
```

```
txtstream.WriteLine("</xsl:template>")
txtstream.WriteLine("</xsl:stylesheet>")
txtstream.Close()


Case "Multi Line Vertical"

txtstream.WriteLine("<?xml version='1.0' encoding='UTF-8'?>")
txtstream.WriteLine("<xsl:stylesheet                              version='1.0'
xmlns:xsl='http://www.w3.org/1999/XSL/Transform'>")
txtstream.WriteLine("<xsl:template match=""/"">")
txtstream.WriteLine("<html>")
txtstream.WriteLine("<head>")
txtstream.WriteLine("<title>Products</title>")
txtstream.WriteLine("<style type='text/css'>")
txtstream.WriteLine("th")
txtstream.WriteLine("{")
txtstream.WriteLine("   COLOR: darkred;")
txtstream.WriteLine("   BACKGROUND-COLOR: white;")
txtstream.WriteLine("   FONT-FAMILY:font-family: Cambria, serif;")
txtstream.WriteLine("   FONT-SIZE: 12px;")
txtstream.WriteLine("   text-align: left;")
txtstream.WriteLine("   white-Space: nowrap;")
txtstream.WriteLine("}")
txtstream.WriteLine("td")
txtstream.WriteLine("{")
txtstream.WriteLine("   COLOR: navy;")
txtstream.WriteLine("   BACKGROUND-COLOR: white;")
txtstream.WriteLine("   FONT-FAMILY: font-family: Cambria, serif;")
txtstream.WriteLine("   FONT-SIZE: 12px;")
txtstream.WriteLine("   text-align: left;")
txtstream.WriteLine("   white-Space: nowrap;")
txtstream.WriteLine("}")
```

```vb
txtstream.WriteLine("</style>")
txtstream.WriteLine("</head>")
txtstream.WriteLine("<body bgcolor='#333333'>")
txtstream.WriteLine("<table colspacing='3' colpadding='3'>")
For Each prop As Object In obj.Properties_
txtstream.WriteLine("<tr><th>" + prop.Name + "</th>")
txtstream.WriteLine("<td><xsl:for-each select=""data/Win32_Process"">")
txtstream.WriteLine("<xsl:value-of select=""" + prop.Name + """/></td>")
txtstream.WriteLine("</xsl:for-each></tr>")
Next
txtstream.WriteLine("</table>")
txtstream.WriteLine("</body>")
txtstream.WriteLine("</html>")
txtstream.WriteLine("</xsl:template>")
txtstream.WriteLine("</xsl:stylesheet>")
txtstream.Close()


End Select


End Sub
```

POPULATE THE

DATAGRIDVIEW

This sub routine populated the DataGridView control with the data supplied in both horizontal and vertical formats. Simply pass in the collection generated by the Return_Management_Collection, specify its orientation and include the name of the DataGridview you want populated.

```
Public Sub Populate_DataGridView(ByVal objs As SWbemObjectSet, ByVal
Orientation As String, ByVal dg As DataGridView)

Dim ob As Object = objs.ItemIndex(0)
dg.Rows.Clear()
dg.Columns.Clear()

Select Case Orientation

Case "Horizontal"

For Each prop As Object In ob.Properties_

dg.Columns.Add(prop.Name, prop.Name)

Next
Dim x As Integer = 0
Dim y As Integer = 0
```

```
For Each obj As Object In objs

dg.Rows.Add()

For Each prop As Object In obj.Properties_

dg.Rows(y).Cells(x).Value = GetValue(prop.Name, obj)
x = x + 1
Next
y = y + 1
x = 0
Next

Case "Vertical"

Dim x As Integer = 0
Dim y As Integer = 0

dg.Columns.Add("Property Name", "Property Name")

For Each obj As Object In objs
dg.Columns.Add("Row" & x, "Row" & x)
x = x + 1
Next

x = 1

For Each prop As Object In ob.Properties_
dg.Rows.Add()
dg.Rows(y).Cells(0).Value = prop.name
For Each obj As Object In objs
dg.Rows(y).Cells(x).Value = GetValue(prop.Name, obj)
x = x + 1
```

```
Next
x = 1
y = y + 1
Next

End Select

End Sub
```

POPULATE THE LISTVIEW

This sub routine populated the ListView control with the data supplied in both horizontal and vertical formats. Simply pass in the collection generated by the Return_Management_Collection, specify its orientation and include the name of the Listview you want populated.

```
Public Sub Populate_Listview(ByVal objs As SWbemObjectSet, ByVal
Orientation As String, ByVal lv As ListView)

Dim ob As Object = objs.ItemIndex(0)
lv.Items.Clear()
lv.Columns.Clear()

Select Case Orientation

Case "Horizontal"

For Each prop As Object In ob.Properties_
lv.Columns.Add(prop.Name)
Next
Dim lI As ListViewItem = Nothing
Dim y As Integer = 0

For Each obj As Object In objs

For Each prop As Object In obj.Properties_
Dim tempstr As String = GetValue(prop.Name, obj)
If y = 0 Then
```

```
lI = lv.Items.Add(tempstr)
y = 1
Else
lI.SubItems.Add(tempstr)
End If
Next
y = 0
Next

Case "Vertical"

Dim x As Integer = 0
Dim y As Integer = 0

lv.Columns.Add("Property Name")

For Each obj As Object In objs
lv.Columns.Add("Row" & x, "Row" & x)
x = x + 1
Next

Dim lI As ListViewItem = Nothing
For Each prop As Object In ob.Properties_
lI = lv.Items.Add(prop.Name)
For Each obj As Object In objs
Dim tempstr As String = GetValue(prop.Name, obj)
lI.SubItems.Add(tempstr)
Next
Next

End Select
```

```
    End Sub

End Module
```

Stylesheets

The difference between boring and oh, wow!

The stylesheets in Appendix A, were used to render these pages. If you find one you like, feel free to use it.

Report:

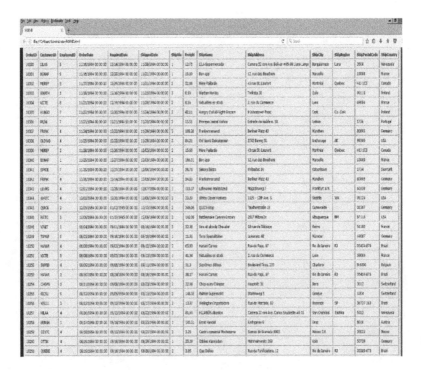

Table

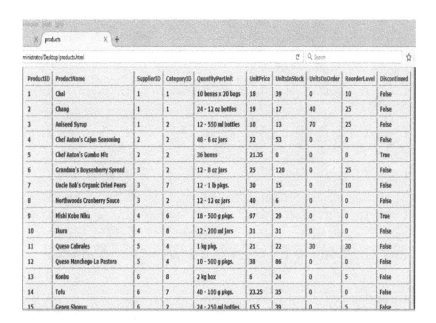

ProductID	ProductName	SupplierID	CategoryID	QuantityPerUnit	UnitPrice	UnitsInStock	UnitsOnOrder	ReorderLevel	Discontinued
1	Chai	1	1	10 boxes x 20 bags	18	39	0	10	False
2	Chang	1	1	24 - 12 oz bottles	19	17	40	25	False
3	Aniseed Syrup	1	2	12 - 550 ml bottles	10	13	70	25	False
4	Chef Anton's Cajun Seasoning	2	2	48 - 6 oz jars	22	53	0	0	False
5	Chef Anton's Gumbo Mix	2	2	36 boxes	21.35	0	0	0	True
6	Grandma's Boysenberry Spread	3	2	12 - 8 oz jars	25	120	0	25	False
7	Uncle Bob's Organic Dried Pears	3	7	12 - 1 lb pkgs.	30	15	0	10	False
8	Northwoods Cranberry Sauce	3	2	12 - 12 oz jars	40	6	0	0	False
9	Mishi Kobe Niku	4	6	18 - 500 g pkgs.	97	29	0	0	True
10	Ikura	4	8	12 - 200 ml jars	31	31	0	0	False
11	Queso Cabrales	5	4	1 kg pkg.	21	22	30	30	False
12	Queso Manchego La Pastora	5	4	10 - 500 g pkgs.	38	86	0	0	False
13	Konbu	6	8	2 kg box	6	24	0	5	False
14	Tofu	6	7	40 - 100 g pkgs.	23.25	35	0	0	False
15	Genen Shoyu	6	2	24 - 250 ml bottles	15.5	39	0	5	False

None:

Black and White

Colored:

AccountExpires	AuthorizationFlags	BadPasswordCount	Caption	CodePage	Comment	CountryCode	Description
			NT AUTHORITY\SYSTEM				Network login profile settings for SYSTEM on NT AUTHORITY
			NT AUTHORITY\LOCAL SERVICE				Network login profile settings for LOCAL SERVICE on NT AUTHORITY
			NT AUTHORITY\NETWORK SERVICE				Network login profile settings for NETWORK SERVICE on NT AUTHORITY
	0	0	Administrator	0	Built-in account for administering the computer/domain	0	Network login profile settings for WIN-S9RLOAKMF3B
			NT SERVICE\SSASTELEMETRY				Network login profile settings for SSASTELEMETRY on NT SERVICE
			NT SERVICE\SSISTELEMETRY350				Network login profile settings for SSISTELEMETRY350 on NT SERVICE
			NT SERVICE\SQLTELEMETRY				Network login profile settings for SQLTELEMETRY on NT SERVICE
			NT SERVICE\MSSQLServerOLAPService				Network login profile settings for MSSQLServerOLAPService on NT SERVICE
			NT SERVICE\ReportServer				Network login profile settings for ReportServer on NT SERVICE
			NT SERVICE\MSSQLFDLauncher				Network login profile settings for MSSQLFDLauncher on NT SERVICE
			NT SERVICE\MSSQLLaunchpad				Network login profile settings for MSSQLLaunchpad on NT SERVICE
			NT SERVICE\MsDtsServer130				Network login profile settings for MsDtsServer130 on NT SERVICE
			NT SERVICE\MSSQLSERVER				Network login profile settings for MSSQLSERVER on NT SERVICE
			IIS APPPOOL\Classic .NET AppPool				Network login profile settings for Classic .NET AppPool on IIS APPPOOL
			IIS APPPOOL\.NET v4.5				Network login profile settings for .NET v4.5 on IIS APPPOOL
			IIS APPPOOL\.NET v2.0				Network login profile settings for .NET v2.0 on IIS APPPOOL
			IIS APPPOOL\.NET v4.5 Classic				Network login profile settings for .NET v4.5 Classic on IIS APPPOOL
			IIS APPPOOL\.NET v2.0 Classic				Network login profile settings for .NET v2.0 Classic on IIS APPPOOL

Oscillating:

Availability	BytesPerSector	Capabilities	CapabilityDescriptions	Caption	CompressionMethod	ConfigManagerErrorCode	ConfigManagerUserConfig
	512	3, 4, 10	Random Access, Supports Writing, SMART Notification	OCZ REVODRIVE350 SCSI Disk Device		0	FALSE
	512	3, 4	Random Access, Supports Writing	NVMe TOSHIBA-RD400		0	FALSE
	512	3, 4, 10	Random Access, Supports Writing, SMART Notification	TOSHIBA DT01ACA200		0	FALSE

3D:

Availability	BytesPerSector	Capabilities	CapabilityDescriptions	Caption	CompressionMethod	ConfigManagerErrorCode	ConfigManagerUserConfig	CreationClassName
	512	3, 4, 10	Random Access, Supports Writing, SMART Notification	OCZ REVODRIVE350 SCSI Disk Device		0	FALSE	Win32_DiskDrive
	512	3, 4	Random Access, Supports Writing	NVMe TOSHIBA-RD400		0	FALSE	Win32_DiskDrive
	512	3, 4, 10	Random Access, Supports Writing, SMART Notification	TOSHIBA DT01ACA200		0	FALSE	Win32_DiskDrive

Shadow Box:

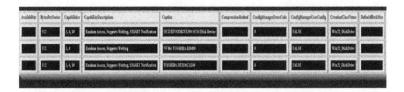

Availability	BytesPerSector	Capabilities	CapabilityDescriptions	Caption	CompressionMethod	ConfigManagerErrorCode	ConfigManagerUserConfig	CreationClassName	DefaultBlockSize
	512	3, 4, 10	Random Access, Supports Writing, SMART Notification	OCZ REVODRIVE350 SCSI Disk Device		0	FALSE	Win32_DiskDrive	
	512	3, 4	Random Access, Supports Writing	NVMe TOSHIBA-RD400		0	FALSE	Win32_DiskDrive	
	512	3, 4, 10	Random Access, Supports Writing, SMART Notification	TOSHIBA DT01ACA200		0	FALSE	Win32_DiskDrive	

Shadow Box Single Line Vertical

BiosCharacteristics	7, 10, 11, 12, 15, 16, 17, 19, 23, 24, 25, 26, 27, 28, 29, 32, 33, 40, 42, 43, 48, 50, 58, 59, 64, 65, 66, 67, 68, 69, 70, 71, 72, 73, 74, 75, 76, 77, 78, 79
BIOSVersion	ALASKA - 1072009, 0504, American Megatrends - 5000C
BuildNumber	
Caption	0504
CodeSet	
CurrentLanguage	en|US|iso8859-1
Description	0504
IdentificationCode	
InstallableLanguages	8
InstallDate	
LanguageEdition	
ListOfLanguages	en|US|iso8859-1, fr|FR|iso8859-1, zh|CN|unicode, , , , ,
Manufacturer	American Megatrends Inc.
Name	0504
OtherTargetOS	
PrimaryBIOS	TRUE

Shadow Box Multi line Vertical

Availability			
BytesPerSector	512	512	512
Capabilities	3, 4, 10	3, 4	3, 4, 10
CapabilityDescriptions	Random Access, Supports Writing, SMART Notification	Random Access, Supports Writing	Random Access, Supports Writing, SMART Notification
Caption	OCZ REVODRIVE350 SCSI Disk Device	NVMe TOSHIBA-RD400	TOSHIBA DT01ACA200
CompressionMethod			
ConfigManagerErrorCode	0		
ConfigManagerUserConfig	FALSE	FALSE	FALSE
CreationClassName	Win32_DiskDrive	Win32_DiskDrive	Win32_DiskDrive
DefaultBlockSize			
Description	Disk drive	Disk drive	Disk drive
DeviceID	\\.\PHYSICALDRIVE2	\\.\PHYSICALDRIVE1	\\.\PHYSICALDRIVE0
ErrorCleared			
ErrorDescription			
ErrorMethodology			
FirmwareRevision	2.59	57CZ4102	MX4OABB0
Index	2	1	0

STYLESHEETS CODE

Decorating your web pages

BELOW ARE SOME STYLESHEETS I COOKED UP THAT I LIKE AND THINK YOU MIGHT TOO. Don't worry I won't be offended if you take and modify to your hearts delight. Please do!

NONE

```
txtstream.WriteLine("<style type='text/css'>")
txtstream.WriteLine("th")
txtstream.WriteLine("{")
txtstream.WriteLine("    COLOR: darkred;")
txtstream.WriteLine("}")
txtstream.WriteLine("td")
txtstream.WriteLine("{")
txtstream.WriteLine("    COLOR: Navy;")
txtstream.WriteLine("}")
txtstream.WriteLine("</style>")
```

BLACK AND WHITE TEXT

```
txtstream.WriteLine("<style type='text/css'>")
txtstream.WriteLine("th")
txtstream.WriteLine("{")
```

```
txtstream.WriteLine("    COLOR: white;")
txtstream.WriteLine("    BACKGROUND-COLOR: black;")
txtstream.WriteLine("    FONT-FAMILY:font-family: Cambria, serif;")
txtstream.WriteLine("    FONT-SIZE: 12px;")
txtstream.WriteLine("    text-align: left;")
txtstream.WriteLine("    white-Space: nowrap;")
txtstream.WriteLine("}")
txtstream.WriteLine("td")
txtstream.WriteLine("{")
txtstream.WriteLine("    COLOR: white;")
txtstream.WriteLine("    BACKGROUND-COLOR: black;")
txtstream.WriteLine("    FONT-FAMILY: font-family: Cambria, serif;")
txtstream.WriteLine("    FONT-SIZE: 12px;")
txtstream.WriteLine("    text-align: left;")
txtstream.WriteLine("    white-Space: nowrap;")
txtstream.WriteLine("}")
txtstream.WriteLine("div")
txtstream.WriteLine("{")
txtstream.WriteLine("    COLOR: white;")
txtstream.WriteLine("    BACKGROUND-COLOR: black;")
txtstream.WriteLine("    FONT-FAMILY: font-family: Cambria, serif;")
txtstream.WriteLine("    FONT-SIZE: 10px;")
txtstream.WriteLine("    text-align: left;")
txtstream.WriteLine("    white-Space: nowrap;")
txtstream.WriteLine("}")
txtstream.WriteLine("span")
txtstream.WriteLine("{")
txtstream.WriteLine("    COLOR: white;")
txtstream.WriteLine("    BACKGROUND-COLOR: black;")
txtstream.WriteLine("    FONT-FAMILY: font-family: Cambria, serif;")
txtstream.WriteLine("    FONT-SIZE: 10px;")
txtstream.WriteLine("    text-align: left;")
txtstream.WriteLine("    white-Space: nowrap;")
```

```
txtstream.WriteLine("    display:inline-block;")
txtstream.WriteLine("    width: 100%;")
txtstream.WriteLine("}")
txtstream.WriteLine("textarea")
txtstream.WriteLine("{")
txtstream.WriteLine("    COLOR: white;")
txtstream.WriteLine("    BACKGROUND-COLOR: black;")
txtstream.WriteLine("    FONT-FAMILY: font-family: Cambria, serif;")
txtstream.WriteLine("    FONT-SIZE: 10px;")
txtstream.WriteLine("    text-align: left;")
txtstream.WriteLine("    white-Space: nowrap;")
txtstream.WriteLine("    width: 100%;")
txtstream.WriteLine("}")
txtstream.WriteLine("select")
txtstream.WriteLine("{")
txtstream.WriteLine("    COLOR: white;")
txtstream.WriteLine("    BACKGROUND-COLOR: black;")
txtstream.WriteLine("    FONT-FAMILY: font-family: Cambria, serif;")
txtstream.WriteLine("    FONT-SIZE: 10px;")
txtstream.WriteLine("    text-align: left;")
txtstream.WriteLine("    white-Space: nowrap;")
txtstream.WriteLine("    width: 100%;")
txtstream.WriteLine("}")
txtstream.WriteLine("input")
txtstream.WriteLine("{")
txtstream.WriteLine("    COLOR: white;")
txtstream.WriteLine("    BACKGROUND-COLOR: black;")
txtstream.WriteLine("    FONT-FAMILY: font-family: Cambria, serif;")
txtstream.WriteLine("    FONT-SIZE: 12px;")
txtstream.WriteLine("    text-align: left;")
txtstream.WriteLine("    display:table-cell;")
txtstream.WriteLine("    white-Space: nowrap;")
txtstream.WriteLine("}")
```

```
txtstream.WriteLine("h1 {")
txtstream.WriteLine("color: antiquewhite;")
txtstream.WriteLine("text-shadow: 1px 1px 1px black;")
txtstream.WriteLine("padding: 3px;")
txtstream.WriteLine("text-align: center;")
txtstream.WriteLine("box-shadow: inset 2px 2px 5px rgba(0,0,0,0.5), inset -2px -2px 5px rgba(255,255,255,0.5)")
txtstream.WriteLine("}")
txtstream.WriteLine("</style>")
```

COLORED TEXT

```
txtstream.WriteLine("<style type='text/css'>")
txtstream.WriteLine("th")
txtstream.WriteLine("{")
txtstream.WriteLine("   COLOR: darkred;")
txtstream.WriteLine("   BACKGROUND-COLOR: #eeeeee;")
txtstream.WriteLine("   FONT-FAMILY:font-family: Cambria, serif;")
txtstream.WriteLine("   FONT-SIZE: 12px;")
txtstream.WriteLine("   text-align: left;")
txtstream.WriteLine("   white-Space: nowrap;")
txtstream.WriteLine("}")
txtstream.WriteLine("td")
txtstream.WriteLine("{")
txtstream.WriteLine("   COLOR: navy;")
txtstream.WriteLine("   BACKGROUND-COLOR: #eeeeee;")
txtstream.WriteLine("   FONT-FAMILY: font-family: Cambria, serif;")
txtstream.WriteLine("   FONT-SIZE: 12px;")
txtstream.WriteLine("   text-align: left;")
txtstream.WriteLine("   white-Space: nowrap;")
txtstream.WriteLine("}")
txtstream.WriteLine("div")
txtstream.WriteLine("{")
```

```
txtstream.WriteLine("    COLOR: white;")
txtstream.WriteLine("    BACKGROUND-COLOR: navy;")
txtstream.WriteLine("    FONT-FAMILY: font-family: Cambria, serif;")
txtstream.WriteLine("    FONT-SIZE: 10px;")
txtstream.WriteLine("    text-align: left;")
txtstream.WriteLine("    white-Space: nowrap;")
txtstream.WriteLine("}")
txtstream.WriteLine("span")
txtstream.WriteLine("{")
txtstream.WriteLine("    COLOR: white;")
txtstream.WriteLine("    BACKGROUND-COLOR: navy;")
txtstream.WriteLine("    FONT-FAMILY: font-family: Cambria, serif;")
txtstream.WriteLine("    FONT-SIZE: 10px;")
txtstream.WriteLine("    text-align: left;")
txtstream.WriteLine("    white-Space: nowrap;")
txtstream.WriteLine("    display:inline-block;")
txtstream.WriteLine("    width: 100%;")
txtstream.WriteLine("}")
txtstream.WriteLine("textarea")
txtstream.WriteLine("{")
txtstream.WriteLine("    COLOR: white;")
txtstream.WriteLine("    BACKGROUND-COLOR: navy;")
txtstream.WriteLine("    FONT-FAMILY: font-family: Cambria, serif;")
txtstream.WriteLine("    FONT-SIZE: 10px;")
txtstream.WriteLine("    text-align: left;")
txtstream.WriteLine("    white-Space: nowrap;")
txtstream.WriteLine("    width: 100%;")
txtstream.WriteLine("}")
txtstream.WriteLine("select")
txtstream.WriteLine("{")
txtstream.WriteLine("    COLOR: white;")
txtstream.WriteLine("    BACKGROUND-COLOR: navy;")
txtstream.WriteLine("    FONT-FAMILY: font-family: Cambria, serif;")
```

```
txtstream.WriteLine("    FONT-SIZE: 10px;")
txtstream.WriteLine("    text-align: left;")
txtstream.WriteLine("    white-Space: nowrap;")
txtstream.WriteLine("    width: 100%;")
txtstream.WriteLine("}")
txtstream.WriteLine("input")
txtstream.WriteLine("{")
txtstream.WriteLine("    COLOR: white;")
txtstream.WriteLine("    BACKGROUND-COLOR: navy;")
txtstream.WriteLine("    FONT-FAMILY: font-family: Cambria, serif;")
txtstream.WriteLine("    FONT-SIZE: 12px;")
txtstream.WriteLine("    text-align: left;")
txtstream.WriteLine("    display:table-cell;")
txtstream.WriteLine("    white-Space: nowrap;")
txtstream.WriteLine("}")
txtstream.WriteLine("h1 {")
txtstream.WriteLine("color: antiquewhite;")
txtstream.WriteLine("text-shadow: 1px 1px 1px black;")
txtstream.WriteLine("padding: 3px;")
txtstream.WriteLine("text-align: center;")
txtstream.WriteLine("box-shadow: inset 2px 2px 5px rgba(0,0,0,0.5), inset -
2px -2px 5px rgba(255,255,255,0.5)")
txtstream.WriteLine("}")
txtstream.WriteLine("</style>")
```

OSCILLATING ROW COLORS

```
txtstream.WriteLine("<style>")
txtstream.WriteLine("th")
txtstream.WriteLine("{")
txtstream.WriteLine("    COLOR: white;")
```

```
txtstream.WriteLine("    BACKGROUND-COLOR: navy;")
txtstream.WriteLine("    FONT-FAMILY:font-family: Cambria, serif;")
txtstream.WriteLine("    FONT-SIZE: 12px;")
txtstream.WriteLine("    text-align: left;")
txtstream.WriteLine("    white-Space: nowrap;")
txtstream.WriteLine("}")
txtstream.WriteLine("td")
txtstream.WriteLine("{")
txtstream.WriteLine("    COLOR: navy;")
txtstream.WriteLine("    FONT-FAMILY: font-family: Cambria, serif;")
txtstream.WriteLine("    FONT-SIZE: 12px;")
txtstream.WriteLine("    text-align: left;")
txtstream.WriteLine("    white-Space: nowrap;")
txtstream.WriteLine("}")
txtstream.WriteLine("div")
txtstream.WriteLine("{")
txtstream.WriteLine("    COLOR: navy;")
txtstream.WriteLine("    FONT-FAMILY: font-family: Cambria, serif;")
txtstream.WriteLine("    FONT-SIZE: 12px;")
txtstream.WriteLine("    text-align: left;")
txtstream.WriteLine("    white-Space: nowrap;")
txtstream.WriteLine("}")
txtstream.WriteLine("span")
txtstream.WriteLine("{")
txtstream.WriteLine("    COLOR: navy;")
txtstream.WriteLine("    FONT-FAMILY: font-family: Cambria, serif;")
txtstream.WriteLine("    FONT-SIZE: 12px;")
txtstream.WriteLine("    text-align: left;")
txtstream.WriteLine("    white-Space: nowrap;")
txtstream.WriteLine("    width: 100%;")
txtstream.WriteLine("}")
txtstream.WriteLine("textarea")
txtstream.WriteLine("{")
```

```
txtstream.WriteLine("   COLOR: navy;")
txtstream.WriteLine("   FONT-FAMILY: font-family: Cambria, serif;")
txtstream.WriteLine("   FONT-SIZE: 12px;")
txtstream.WriteLine("   text-align: left;")
txtstream.WriteLine("   white-Space: nowrap;")
txtstream.WriteLine("   display:inline-block;")
txtstream.WriteLine("   width: 100%;")
txtstream.WriteLine("}")
txtstream.WriteLine("select")
txtstream.WriteLine("{")
txtstream.WriteLine("   COLOR: navy;")
txtstream.WriteLine("   FONT-FAMILY: font-family: Cambria, serif;")
txtstream.WriteLine("   FONT-SIZE: 10px;")
txtstream.WriteLine("   text-align: left;")
txtstream.WriteLine("   white-Space: nowrap;")
txtstream.WriteLine("   display:inline-block;")
txtstream.WriteLine("   width: 100%;")
txtstream.WriteLine("}")
txtstream.WriteLine("input")
txtstream.WriteLine("{")
txtstream.WriteLine("   COLOR: navy;")
txtstream.WriteLine("   FONT-FAMILY: font-family: Cambria, serif;")
txtstream.WriteLine("   FONT-SIZE: 12px;")
txtstream.WriteLine("   text-align: left;")
txtstream.WriteLine("   display:table-cell;")
txtstream.WriteLine("   white-Space: nowrap;")
txtstream.WriteLine("}")
txtstream.WriteLine("h1 {")
txtstream.WriteLine("color: antiquewhite;")
txtstream.WriteLine("text-shadow: 1px 1px 1px black;")
txtstream.WriteLine("padding: 3px;")
txtstream.WriteLine("text-align: center;")
```

```
txtstream.WriteLine("box-shadow: inset 2px 2px 5px rgba(0,0,0,0.5), inset -
2px -2px 5px rgba(255,255,255,0.5)")
txtstream.WriteLine("}")
txtstream.WriteLine("tr:nth-child(even){background-color:#f2f2f2;}")
txtstream.WriteLine("tr:nth-child(odd){background-color:#cccccc;
color:#f2f2f2;}")
txtstream.WriteLine("</style>")
```

GHOST DECORATED

```
txtstream.WriteLine("<style type='text/css'>")
txtstream.WriteLine("th")
txtstream.WriteLine("{")
txtstream.WriteLine("   COLOR: black;")
txtstream.WriteLine("   BACKGROUND-COLOR: white;")
txtstream.WriteLine("   FONT-FAMILY:font-family: Cambria, serif;")
txtstream.WriteLine("   FONT-SIZE: 12px;")
txtstream.WriteLine("   text-align: left;")
txtstream.WriteLine("   white-Space: nowrap;")
txtstream.WriteLine("}")
txtstream.WriteLine("td")
txtstream.WriteLine("{")
txtstream.WriteLine("   COLOR: black;")
txtstream.WriteLine("   BACKGROUND-COLOR: white;")
txtstream.WriteLine("   FONT-FAMILY: font-family: Cambria, serif;")
txtstream.WriteLine("   FONT-SIZE: 12px;")
txtstream.WriteLine("   text-align: left;")
txtstream.WriteLine("   white-Space: nowrap;")
txtstream.WriteLine("}")
txtstream.WriteLine("div")
txtstream.WriteLine("{")
txtstream.WriteLine("   COLOR: black;")
txtstream.WriteLine("   BACKGROUND-COLOR: white;")
```

```
txtstream.WriteLine("    FONT-FAMILY: font-family: Cambria, serif;")
txtstream.WriteLine("    FONT-SIZE: 10px;")
txtstream.WriteLine("    text-align: left;")
txtstream.WriteLine("    white-Space: nowrap;")
txtstream.WriteLine("}")
txtstream.WriteLine("span")
txtstream.WriteLine("{")
txtstream.WriteLine("    COLOR: black;")
txtstream.WriteLine("    BACKGROUND-COLOR: white;")
txtstream.WriteLine("    FONT-FAMILY: font-family: Cambria, serif;")
txtstream.WriteLine("    FONT-SIZE: 10px;")
txtstream.WriteLine("    text-align: left;")
txtstream.WriteLine("    white-Space: nowrap;")
txtstream.WriteLine("    display:inline-block;")
txtstream.WriteLine("    width: 100%;")
txtstream.WriteLine("}")
txtstream.WriteLine("textarea")
txtstream.WriteLine("{")
txtstream.WriteLine("    COLOR: black;")
txtstream.WriteLine("    BACKGROUND-COLOR: white;")
txtstream.WriteLine("    FONT-FAMILY: font-family: Cambria, serif;")
txtstream.WriteLine("    FONT-SIZE: 10px;")
txtstream.WriteLine("    text-align: left;")
txtstream.WriteLine("    white-Space: nowrap;")
txtstream.WriteLine("    width: 100%;")
txtstream.WriteLine("}")
txtstream.WriteLine("select")
txtstream.WriteLine("{")
txtstream.WriteLine("    COLOR: black;")
txtstream.WriteLine("    BACKGROUND-COLOR: white;")
txtstream.WriteLine("    FONT-FAMILY: font-family: Cambria, serif;")
txtstream.WriteLine("    FONT-SIZE: 10px;")
txtstream.WriteLine("    text-align: left;")
```

```
txtstream.WriteLine("   white-Space: nowrap;")
txtstream.WriteLine("   width: 100%;")
txtstream.WriteLine("}")
txtstream.WriteLine("input")
txtstream.WriteLine("{")
txtstream.WriteLine("   COLOR: black;")
txtstream.WriteLine("   BACKGROUND-COLOR: white;")
txtstream.WriteLine("   FONT-FAMILY: font-family: Cambria, serif;")
txtstream.WriteLine("   FONT-SIZE: 12px;")
txtstream.WriteLine("   text-align: left;")
txtstream.WriteLine("   display:table-cell;")
txtstream.WriteLine("   white-Space: nowrap;")
txtstream.WriteLine("}")
txtstream.WriteLine("h1 {")
txtstream.WriteLine("color: antiquewhite;")
txtstream.WriteLine("text-shadow: 1px 1px 1px black;")
txtstream.WriteLine("padding: 3px;")
txtstream.WriteLine("text-align: center;")
txtstream.WriteLine("box-shadow: inset 2px 2px 5px rgba(0,0,0,0.5), inset -2px -2px 5px rgba(255,255,255,0.5)")
txtstream.WriteLine("}")
txtstream.WriteLine("</style>")
```

3D


```
txtstream.WriteLine("<style type='text/css'>")
txtstream.WriteLine("body")
txtstream.WriteLine("{")
txtstream.WriteLine("   PADDING-RIGHT: 0px;")
txtstream.WriteLine("   PADDING-LEFT: 0px;")
txtstream.WriteLine("   PADDING-BOTTOM: 0px;")
txtstream.WriteLine("   MARGIN: 0px;")
```

```
txtstream.WriteLine("    COLOR: #333;")
txtstream.WriteLine("    PADDING-TOP: 0px;")
txtstream.WriteLine("    FONT-FAMILY: verdana, arial, helvetica, sans-serif;")
txtstream.WriteLine("}")
txtstream.WriteLine("table")
txtstream.WriteLine("{")
txtstream.WriteLine("    BORDER-RIGHT: #999999 3px solid;")
txtstream.WriteLine("    PADDING-RIGHT: 6px;")
txtstream.WriteLine("    PADDING-LEFT: 6px;")
txtstream.WriteLine("    FONT-WEIGHT: Bold;")
txtstream.WriteLine("    FONT-SIZE: 14px;")
txtstream.WriteLine("    PADDING-BOTTOM: 6px;")
txtstream.WriteLine("    COLOR: Peru;")
txtstream.WriteLine("    LINE-HEIGHT: 14px;")
txtstream.WriteLine("    PADDING-TOP: 6px;")
txtstream.WriteLine("    BORDER-BOTTOM: #999 1px solid;")
txtstream.WriteLine("    BACKGROUND-COLOR: #eeeeee;")
txtstream.WriteLine("    FONT-FAMILY: verdana, arial, helvetica, sans-serif;")
txtstream.WriteLine("    FONT-SIZE: 12px;")
txtstream.WriteLine("}")
txtstream.WriteLine("th")
txtstream.WriteLine("{")
txtstream.WriteLine("    BORDER-RIGHT: #999999 3px solid;")
txtstream.WriteLine("    PADDING-RIGHT: 6px;")
txtstream.WriteLine("    PADDING-LEFT: 6px;")
txtstream.WriteLine("    FONT-WEIGHT: Bold;")
txtstream.WriteLine("    FONT-SIZE: 14px;")
txtstream.WriteLine("    PADDING-BOTTOM: 6px;")
txtstream.WriteLine("    COLOR: darkred;")
txtstream.WriteLine("    LINE-HEIGHT: 14px;")
txtstream.WriteLine("    PADDING-TOP: 6px;")
txtstream.WriteLine("    BORDER-BOTTOM: #999 1px solid;")
txtstream.WriteLine("    BACKGROUND-COLOR: #eeeeee;")
```

```
txtstream.WriteLine("    FONT-FAMILY:font-family: Cambria, serif;")
txtstream.WriteLine("    FONT-SIZE: 12px;")
txtstream.WriteLine("    text-align: left;")
txtstream.WriteLine("    white-Space: nowrap;")
txtstream.WriteLine("}")
txtstream.WriteLine(".th")
txtstream.WriteLine("{")
txtstream.WriteLine("    BORDER-RIGHT: #999999 2px solid;")
txtstream.WriteLine("    PADDING-RIGHT: 6px;")
txtstream.WriteLine("    PADDING-LEFT: 6px;")
txtstream.WriteLine("    FONT-WEIGHT: Bold;")
txtstream.WriteLine("    PADDING-BOTTOM: 6px;")
txtstream.WriteLine("    COLOR: black;")
txtstream.WriteLine("    PADDING-TOP: 6px;")
txtstream.WriteLine("    BORDER-BOTTOM: #999 2px solid;")
txtstream.WriteLine("    BACKGROUND-COLOR: #eeeeee;")
txtstream.WriteLine("    FONT-FAMILY: font-family: Cambria, serif;")
txtstream.WriteLine("    FONT-SIZE: 10px;")
txtstream.WriteLine("    text-align: right;")
txtstream.WriteLine("    white-Space: nowrap;")
txtstream.WriteLine("}")
txtstream.WriteLine("td")
txtstream.WriteLine("{")
txtstream.WriteLine("    BORDER-RIGHT: #999999 3px solid;")
txtstream.WriteLine("    PADDING-RIGHT: 6px;")
txtstream.WriteLine("    PADDING-LEFT: 6px;")
txtstream.WriteLine("    FONT-WEIGHT: Normal;")
txtstream.WriteLine("    PADDING-BOTTOM: 6px;")
txtstream.WriteLine("    COLOR: navy;")
txtstream.WriteLine("    LINE-HEIGHT: 14px;")
txtstream.WriteLine("    PADDING-TOP: 6px;")
txtstream.WriteLine("    BORDER-BOTTOM: #999 1px solid;")
txtstream.WriteLine("    BACKGROUND-COLOR: #eeeeee;")
```

```
txtstream.WriteLine("    FONT-FAMILY: font-family: Cambria, serif;")
txtstream.WriteLine("    FONT-SIZE: 12px;")
txtstream.WriteLine("    text-align: left;")
txtstream.WriteLine("    white-Space: nowrap;")
txtstream.WriteLine("}")
txtstream.WriteLine("div")
txtstream.WriteLine("{")
txtstream.WriteLine("    BORDER-RIGHT: #999999 3px solid;")
txtstream.WriteLine("    PADDING-RIGHT: 6px;")
txtstream.WriteLine("    PADDING-LEFT: 6px;")
txtstream.WriteLine("    FONT-WEIGHT: Normal;")
txtstream.WriteLine("    PADDING-BOTTOM: 6px;")
txtstream.WriteLine("    COLOR: white;")
txtstream.WriteLine("    PADDING-TOP: 6px;")
txtstream.WriteLine("    BORDER-BOTTOM: #999 1px solid;")
txtstream.WriteLine("    BACKGROUND-COLOR: navy;")
txtstream.WriteLine("    FONT-FAMILY: font-family: Cambria, serif;")
txtstream.WriteLine("    FONT-SIZE: 10px;")
txtstream.WriteLine("    text-align: left;")
txtstream.WriteLine("    white-Space: nowrap;")
txtstream.WriteLine("}")
txtstream.WriteLine("span")
txtstream.WriteLine("{")
txtstream.WriteLine("    BORDER-RIGHT: #999999 3px solid;")
txtstream.WriteLine("    PADDING-RIGHT: 3px;")
txtstream.WriteLine("    PADDING-LEFT: 3px;")
txtstream.WriteLine("    FONT-WEIGHT: Normal;")
txtstream.WriteLine("    PADDING-BOTTOM: 3px;")
txtstream.WriteLine("    COLOR: white;")
txtstream.WriteLine("    PADDING-TOP: 3px;")
txtstream.WriteLine("    BORDER-BOTTOM: #999 1px solid;")
txtstream.WriteLine("    BACKGROUND-COLOR: navy;")
txtstream.WriteLine("    FONT-FAMILY: font-family: Cambria, serif;")
```

```
txtstream.WriteLine("    FONT-SIZE: 10px;")
txtstream.WriteLine("    text-align: left;")
txtstream.WriteLine("    white-Space: nowrap;")
txtstream.WriteLine("    display:inline-block;")
txtstream.WriteLine("    width: 100%;")
txtstream.WriteLine("}")
txtstream.WriteLine("textarea")
txtstream.WriteLine("{")
txtstream.WriteLine("    BORDER-RIGHT: #999999 3px solid;")
txtstream.WriteLine("    PADDING-RIGHT: 3px;")
txtstream.WriteLine("    PADDING-LEFT: 3px;")
txtstream.WriteLine("    FONT-WEIGHT: Normal;")
txtstream.WriteLine("    PADDING-BOTTOM: 3px;")
txtstream.WriteLine("    COLOR: white;")
txtstream.WriteLine("    PADDING-TOP: 3px;")
txtstream.WriteLine("    BORDER-BOTTOM: #999 1px solid;")
txtstream.WriteLine("    BACKGROUND-COLOR: navy;")
txtstream.WriteLine("    FONT-FAMILY: font-family: Cambria, serif;")
txtstream.WriteLine("    FONT-SIZE: 10px;")
txtstream.WriteLine("    text-align: left;")
txtstream.WriteLine("    white-Space: nowrap;")
txtstream.WriteLine("    width: 100%;")
txtstream.WriteLine("}")
txtstream.WriteLine("select")
txtstream.WriteLine("{")
txtstream.WriteLine("    BORDER-RIGHT: #999999 3px solid;")
txtstream.WriteLine("    PADDING-RIGHT: 6px;")
txtstream.WriteLine("    PADDING-LEFT: 6px;")
txtstream.WriteLine("    FONT-WEIGHT: Normal;")
txtstream.WriteLine("    PADDING-BOTTOM: 6px;")
txtstream.WriteLine("    COLOR: white;")
txtstream.WriteLine("    PADDING-TOP: 6px;")
txtstream.WriteLine("    BORDER-BOTTOM: #999 1px solid;")
```

```
txtstream.WriteLine("   BACKGROUND-COLOR: navy;")
txtstream.WriteLine("   FONT-FAMILY: font-family: Cambria, serif;")
txtstream.WriteLine("   FONT-SIZE: 10px;")
txtstream.WriteLine("   text-align: left;")
txtstream.WriteLine("   white-Space: nowrap;")
txtstream.WriteLine("   width: 100%;")
txtstream.WriteLine("}")
txtstream.WriteLine("input")
txtstream.WriteLine("{")
txtstream.WriteLine("   BORDER-RIGHT: #999999 3px solid;")
txtstream.WriteLine("   PADDING-RIGHT: 3px;")
txtstream.WriteLine("   PADDING-LEFT: 3px;")
txtstream.WriteLine("   FONT-WEIGHT: Bold;")
txtstream.WriteLine("   PADDING-BOTTOM: 3px;")
txtstream.WriteLine("   COLOR: white;")
txtstream.WriteLine("   PADDING-TOP: 3px;")
txtstream.WriteLine("   BORDER-BOTTOM: #999 1px solid;")
txtstream.WriteLine("   BACKGROUND-COLOR: navy;")
txtstream.WriteLine("   FONT-FAMILY: font-family: Cambria, serif;")
txtstream.WriteLine("   FONT-SIZE: 12px;")
txtstream.WriteLine("   text-align: left;")
txtstream.WriteLine("   display:table-cell;")
txtstream.WriteLine("   white-Space: nowrap;")
txtstream.WriteLine("   width: 100%;")
txtstream.WriteLine("}")
txtstream.WriteLine("h1 {")
txtstream.WriteLine("color: antiquewhite;")
txtstream.WriteLine("text-shadow: 1px 1px 1px black;")
txtstream.WriteLine("padding: 3px;")
txtstream.WriteLine("text-align: center;")
txtstream.WriteLine("box-shadow: inset 2px 2px 5px rgba(0,0,0,0.5), inset -
2px -2px 5px rgba(255,255,255,0.5)")
txtstream.WriteLine("}")
```

txtstream.WriteLine("</style>")

SHADOW BOX

txtstream.WriteLine("<style type='text/css'>")

txtstream.WriteLine("body")

txtstream.WriteLine("{")

txtstream.WriteLine("   PADDING-RIGHT: 0px;")

txtstream.WriteLine("   PADDING-LEFT: 0px;")

txtstream.WriteLine("   PADDING-BOTTOM: 0px;")

txtstream.WriteLine("   MARGIN: 0px;")

txtstream.WriteLine("   COLOR: #333;")

txtstream.WriteLine("   PADDING-TOP: 0px;")

txtstream.WriteLine("   FONT-FAMILY: verdana, arial, helvetica, sans-serif;")

txtstream.WriteLine("}")

txtstream.WriteLine("table")

txtstream.WriteLine("{")

txtstream.WriteLine("   BORDER-RIGHT: #999999 1px solid;")

txtstream.WriteLine("   PADDING-RIGHT: 1px;")

txtstream.WriteLine("   PADDING-LEFT: 1px;")

txtstream.WriteLine("   PADDING-BOTTOM: 1px;")

txtstream.WriteLine("   LINE-HEIGHT: 8px;")

txtstream.WriteLine("   PADDING-TOP: 1px;")

txtstream.WriteLine("   BORDER-BOTTOM: #999 1px solid;")

txtstream.WriteLine("   BACKGROUND-COLOR: #eeeeee;")

txtstream.WriteLine("
filter:progid:DXImageTransform.Microsoft.Shadow(color='silver',   Direction=135, Strength=16)")

txtstream.WriteLine("}")

txtstream.WriteLine("th")

txtstream.WriteLine("{")

txtstream.WriteLine("   BORDER-RIGHT: #999999 3px solid;")

txtstream.WriteLine("   PADDING-RIGHT: 6px;")

```
txtstream.WriteLine("    PADDING-LEFT: 6px;")
txtstream.WriteLine("    FONT-WEIGHT: Bold;")
txtstream.WriteLine("    FONT-SIZE: 14px;")
txtstream.WriteLine("    PADDING-BOTTOM: 6px;")
txtstream.WriteLine("    COLOR: darkred;")
txtstream.WriteLine("    LINE-HEIGHT: 14px;")
txtstream.WriteLine("    PADDING-TOP: 6px;")
txtstream.WriteLine("    BORDER-BOTTOM: #999 1px solid;")
txtstream.WriteLine("    BACKGROUND-COLOR: #eeeeee;")
txtstream.WriteLine("    FONT-FAMILY: font-family: Cambria, serif;")
txtstream.WriteLine("    FONT-SIZE: 12px;")
txtstream.WriteLine("    text-align: left;")
txtstream.WriteLine("    white-Space: nowrap;")
txtstream.WriteLine("}")
txtstream.WriteLine(".th")
txtstream.WriteLine("{")
txtstream.WriteLine("    BORDER-RIGHT: #999999 2px solid;")
txtstream.WriteLine("    PADDING-RIGHT: 6px;")
txtstream.WriteLine("    PADDING-LEFT: 6px;")
txtstream.WriteLine("    FONT-WEIGHT: Bold;")
txtstream.WriteLine("    PADDING-BOTTOM: 6px;")
txtstream.WriteLine("    COLOR: black;")
txtstream.WriteLine("    PADDING-TOP: 6px;")
txtstream.WriteLine("    BORDER-BOTTOM: #999 2px solid;")
txtstream.WriteLine("    BACKGROUND-COLOR: #eeeeee;")
txtstream.WriteLine("    FONT-FAMILY: font-family: Cambria, serif;")
txtstream.WriteLine("    FONT-SIZE: 10px;")
txtstream.WriteLine("    text-align: right;")
txtstream.WriteLine("    white-Space: nowrap;")
txtstream.WriteLine("}")
txtstream.WriteLine("td")
txtstream.WriteLine("{")
txtstream.WriteLine("    BORDER-RIGHT: #999999 3px solid;")
```

```
txtstream.WriteLine("   PADDING-RIGHT: 6px;")
txtstream.WriteLine("   PADDING-LEFT: 6px;")
txtstream.WriteLine("   FONT-WEIGHT: Normal;")
txtstream.WriteLine("   PADDING-BOTTOM: 6px;")
txtstream.WriteLine("   COLOR: navy;")
txtstream.WriteLine("   LINE-HEIGHT: 14px;")
txtstream.WriteLine("   PADDING-TOP: 6px;")
txtstream.WriteLine("   BORDER-BOTTOM: #999 1px solid;")
txtstream.WriteLine("   BACKGROUND-COLOR: #eeeeee;")
txtstream.WriteLine("   FONT-FAMILY: font-family: Cambria, serif;")
txtstream.WriteLine("   FONT-SIZE: 12px;")
txtstream.WriteLine("   text-align: left;")
txtstream.WriteLine("   white-Space: nowrap;")
txtstream.WriteLine("}")
txtstream.WriteLine("div")
txtstream.WriteLine("{")
txtstream.WriteLine("   BORDER-RIGHT: #999999 3px solid;")
txtstream.WriteLine("   PADDING-RIGHT: 6px;")
txtstream.WriteLine("   PADDING-LEFT: 6px;")
txtstream.WriteLine("   FONT-WEIGHT: Normal;")
txtstream.WriteLine("   PADDING-BOTTOM: 6px;")
txtstream.WriteLine("   COLOR: white;")
txtstream.WriteLine("   PADDING-TOP: 6px;")
txtstream.WriteLine("   BORDER-BOTTOM: #999 1px solid;")
txtstream.WriteLine("   BACKGROUND-COLOR: navy;")
txtstream.WriteLine("   FONT-FAMILY: font-family: Cambria, serif;")
txtstream.WriteLine("   FONT-SIZE: 10px;")
txtstream.WriteLine("   text-align: left;")
txtstream.WriteLine("   white-Space: nowrap;")
txtstream.WriteLine("}")
txtstream.WriteLine("span")
txtstream.WriteLine("{")
txtstream.WriteLine("   BORDER-RIGHT: #999999 3px solid;")
```

```
txtstream.WriteLine("    PADDING-RIGHT: 3px;")
txtstream.WriteLine("    PADDING-LEFT: 3px;")
txtstream.WriteLine("    FONT-WEIGHT: Normal;")
txtstream.WriteLine("    PADDING-BOTTOM: 3px;")
txtstream.WriteLine("    COLOR: white;")
txtstream.WriteLine("    PADDING-TOP: 3px;")
txtstream.WriteLine("    BORDER-BOTTOM: #999 1px solid;")
txtstream.WriteLine("    BACKGROUND-COLOR: navy;")
txtstream.WriteLine("    FONT-FAMILY: font-family: Cambria, serif;")
txtstream.WriteLine("    FONT-SIZE: 10px;")
txtstream.WriteLine("    text-align: left;")
txtstream.WriteLine("    white-Space: nowrap;")
txtstream.WriteLine("    display: inline-block;")
txtstream.WriteLine("    width: 100%;")
txtstream.WriteLine("}")
txtstream.WriteLine("textarea")
txtstream.WriteLine("{")
txtstream.WriteLine("    BORDER-RIGHT: #999999 3px solid;")
txtstream.WriteLine("    PADDING-RIGHT: 3px;")
txtstream.WriteLine("    PADDING-LEFT: 3px;")
txtstream.WriteLine("    FONT-WEIGHT: Normal;")
txtstream.WriteLine("    PADDING-BOTTOM: 3px;")
txtstream.WriteLine("    COLOR: white;")
txtstream.WriteLine("    PADDING-TOP: 3px;")
txtstream.WriteLine("    BORDER-BOTTOM: #999 1px solid;")
txtstream.WriteLine("    BACKGROUND-COLOR: navy;")
txtstream.WriteLine("    FONT-FAMILY: font-family: Cambria, serif;")
txtstream.WriteLine("    FONT-SIZE: 10px;")
txtstream.WriteLine("    text-align: left;")
txtstream.WriteLine("    white-Space: nowrap;")
txtstream.WriteLine("    width: 100%;")
txtstream.WriteLine("}")
txtstream.WriteLine("select")
```

```
txtstream.WriteLine("{")
txtstream.WriteLine("   BORDER-RIGHT: #999999 3px solid;")
txtstream.WriteLine("   PADDING-RIGHT: 6px;")
txtstream.WriteLine("   PADDING-LEFT: 6px;")
txtstream.WriteLine("   FONT-WEIGHT: Normal;")
txtstream.WriteLine("   PADDING-BOTTOM: 6px;")
txtstream.WriteLine("   COLOR: white;")
txtstream.WriteLine("   PADDING-TOP: 6px;")
txtstream.WriteLine("   BORDER-BOTTOM: #999 1px solid;")
txtstream.WriteLine("   BACKGROUND-COLOR: navy;")
txtstream.WriteLine("   FONT-FAMILY: font-family: Cambria, serif;")
txtstream.WriteLine("   FONT-SIZE: 10px;")
txtstream.WriteLine("   text-align: left;")
txtstream.WriteLine("   white-Space: nowrap;")
txtstream.WriteLine("   width: 100%;")
txtstream.WriteLine("}")
txtstream.WriteLine("input")
txtstream.WriteLine("{")
txtstream.WriteLine("   BORDER-RIGHT: #999999 3px solid;")
txtstream.WriteLine("   PADDING-RIGHT: 3px;")
txtstream.WriteLine("   PADDING-LEFT: 3px;")
txtstream.WriteLine("   FONT-WEIGHT: Bold;")
txtstream.WriteLine("   PADDING-BOTTOM: 3px;")
txtstream.WriteLine("   COLOR: white;")
txtstream.WriteLine("   PADDING-TOP: 3px;")
txtstream.WriteLine("   BORDER-BOTTOM: #999 1px solid;")
txtstream.WriteLine("   BACKGROUND-COLOR: navy;")
txtstream.WriteLine("   FONT-FAMILY: font-family: Cambria, serif;")
txtstream.WriteLine("   FONT-SIZE: 12px;")
txtstream.WriteLine("   text-align: left;")
txtstream.WriteLine("   display: table-cell;")
txtstream.WriteLine("   white-Space: nowrap;")
txtstream.WriteLine("   width: 100%;")
```

```
txtstream.WriteLine("}")
txtstream.WriteLine("h1 {")
txtstream.WriteLine("color: antiquewhite;")
txtstream.WriteLine("text-shadow: 1px 1px 1px black;")
txtstream.WriteLine("padding: 3px;")
txtstream.WriteLine("text-align: center;")
txtstream.WriteLine("box-shadow: inset 2px 2px 5px rgba(0,0,0,0.5), inset -2px -2px 5px rgba(255,255,255,0.5)")
txtstream.WriteLine("}")
txtstream.WriteLine("</style>")
```

www.ingramcontent.com/pod-product-compliance
Lightning Source LLC
LaVergne TN
LVHW041215050326
832903LV00021B/636